Rupert Thomson
Critical Essays

GYLPHI CONTEMPORARY WRITERS: CRITICAL ESSAYS

SERIES EDITOR: SARAH DILLON

Gylphi Contemporary Writers: Critical Essays presents a new approach to the academic study of living authors. The titles in this series are devoted to contemporary British, Irish and American authors whose work is popularly and critically valued but on whom a significant body of academic work has yet to be established. Each of the titles in this series is developed out of the best contributions to an international conference on its author; represents the most intelligent and provocative material in current thinking about that author's work; and, suggests future avenues of thought, comparison and analysis. With each title prefaced by an author foreword, this series embraces the challenges of writing on living authors and provides the foundation stones for future critical work on significant contemporary writers.

Series Titles

David Mitchell: Critical Essays (2011)
Edited by Sarah Dillon. Foreword by David Mitchell.

Maggie Gee: Critical Essays (2015)
Edited by Sarah Dillon and Caroline Edwards. Foreword by Maggie Gee.

China Miéville: Critical Essays (2015)
Edited by Caroline Edwards and Tony Venezia. Foreword by China Miéville.

Adam Roberts: Critical Essays (2016)
Edited by Christos Callow Jr. and Anna McFarlane. Foreword by Adam Roberts.

Rupert Thomson: Critical Essays (2016)
Edited by Rebecca Pohl and Christopher Vardy. Foreword by Rupert Thomson.

Tom McCarthy: Critical Essays (2016)
Edited by Dennis Duncan. Foreword by Tom McCarthy.

Rupert Thomson
Critical Essays

edited by
Rebecca Pohl and Christopher Vardy

Gylphi

A *Gylphi Limited* Book

First published in Great Britain in 2016
by Gylphi Limited

Copyright © Gylphi Limited, 2016

A CIP catalogue record for this book is available from the British Library.

ISBN 978-1-78024-057-2 (pbk)
ISBN 978-1-78024-058-9 (Kindle)
ISBN 978-1-78024-059-6 (EPUB)

Design and typesetting by Gylphi Limited. Printed in the UK by imprintdigital. com, Exeter.

Gylphi Limited
PO Box 993
Canterbury CT1 9EP, UK

Don't forget Note refs index

Contents

Acknowledgements

Enormous thanks for time and enthusiasm are due first and foremost to Rupert Thomson himself, who braved a room full of academics discussing his work and then, through his gracious and incisive contributions, made our conversations so much stronger. We are especially grateful to him for introducing the collection with such a beautiful foreword, which adds the writer's perspective to the scholarship at play.

We are also very grateful to Sarah Dillon, our series editor, for having initiated this much-needed series focusing on contemporary writers, and more specifically for her patience with and conviction in our collection, as well as her advice along the way. Our gratitude also goes to our publisher, Gylphi, for the sustained support over the course of this publication.

This volume comes out of a conference dedicated to Rupert Thomson's writing held in Manchester in June 2013. We would like to thank the Centre for New Writing Manchester, the SALC Graduate School, and GRANTA for sponsoring the event, as well as Waterstones Deansgate and the John Rylands Library Deansgate for generously opening up their events spaces to us.

It has been a real pleasure collaborating with the excellent contributors assembled in this volume, whose chapters are full of insight and rigour and speak so eloquently for the richness of Thomson's work.

Finally, thank you to Kaye Mitchell for recommending the beautiful strangeness of Thomson's prose and so getting the ball rolling, before anybody even knew there would be a ball. And to Iain Bailey, for all the help with detail.

Rebecca Pohl and Christopher Vardy, Manchester 2015

List of Abbreviations

Abbreviations of works cited by Rupert Thomson.

Date of first publication is in parenthesis, followed by details of edition cited throughout (if different from original edition).

DL   *Dreams of Leaving* (1987). London: Bloomsbury.

FGH   *The Five Gates of Hell* (1991). London: Bloomsbury.

AF   *Air and Fire* (1994). London: Penguin.

I   *The Insult* (1996). London: Bloomsbury.

S   *Soft!* (1998). London: Bloomsbury.

BR   *The Book of Revelation* (1999). London: Bloomsbury.

DK   *Divided Kingdom* (2005). London: Bloomsbury.

DM   *Death of a Murderer* (2007). London: Bloomsbury.

PGS   *This Party's Got to Stop* (2010). London: Granta.

Se   *Secrecy* (2013). London: Granta.

KC   *Katherine Carlyle* (2015). London: Corsair.

Foreword

Rupert Thomson

I wrote the first draft of my latest novel, *Katherine Carlyle*, as I write all my first drafts: flat out, and free of all restraints. It is a headlong plunge into the unknown each time, with no framework, no plan, no end in sight. As Flannery O'Connor put it: 'I'm like a hound dog; I follow the scent.' And sometimes that is all there is – a scent. It is exhilarating to write into your own apparent ignorance. Somebody once asked W. H. Auden if it was true that you can only write what you know. 'Yes,' he said. 'But you don't know what you know until you write it.' I set off into the dark to see what I can come back with. Structure, background, continuity – all that comes later. I'm with the French artist, Louise Bourgeois, on this: 'I trust my unconscious. My unconscious is my friend.' I'm trying to pin down some kind of psychological truth. I'm after an undertow – the flow of something fresh and unexpected. There's no need to be afraid, or even wary. No one will ever see my first attempt. I have a number of metaphors for how this process feels. I'm a sculptor with a lump of marble. I'm a driver on a motorway at night who turns his headlights off. I'm an actor, but without an audience. I chip away at something formless. I can't seem to remember any of my lines. I take wrong turnings, scenic routes. I get lost. I crash. But somehow I make progress. The marble gradually resolves itself into a shape. My characters slowly come alive. When day dawns and the road appears I'm never where I thought I would be. The journey is always unpredictable. There is always risk, exhilaration, mystery, and panic. There is also, hopefully, the discovery of something that feels both recognizable and new.

While my first draft is one hundred per cent intuitive, my final draft is likely to be one hundred per cent rational. During the writing of a book I move inexorably from one part of myself to another. By the end, ideally, I have become my own most ruthless critic. There are conscious intentions and effects, but there are also connections and resonances that occur at a subconscious level, out of my control, beyond my knowing. Louise Bourgeois again: 'The meaning of things is not always clear at the beginning. It becomes apparent when the work is done.' It is only when I am publicising a book that I begin to understand what it is that I have written. By then, the making of that particular book will have become a distant memory. At least a year will have gone by. Maybe more. And that distance is useful. Instructive. The Russian film-maker, Andrei Tarkovsky, famously said that 'a book read by a thousand different people is a thousand different books.' Just as a book is the sole property of the writer during the writing, so it becomes the sole property of the reader once it has been written. There is a pleasing symmetry about this transfer of ownership. I'm removed from the equation. The book replaces me. These days, though I am questioned, as most writers are, by audiences at literary festivals or by journalists, I often have the feeling that I'm no longer an authority. I'm just another reader with ideas about something I have read. How intriguing, then, to be invited to the John Rylands Library in Manchester on June 17th 2013 to listen to a gathering of academics deliver papers on my work. When the day came, I was impressed by the variety and depth of the various approaches and responses. I agreed with some, disagreed with others. I was startled, humbled, mystified, amused. As I sat there as unobtrusively as possible, in the back row, Tarkovsky's words came back to me. Each of the people talking was an authority in his or her own right. Everything that was being said had absolute validity.

It was a privilege and an honour to attend the symposium, but I'm not sure I could make a habit of it. If I have a reputation at all, it is for producing a different novel every time – critics have compared me to Kafka, J. G. Ballard, Angela Carter, Dickens, Elmore Leonard, Gabriel Garcia Marquez, and Mervyn Peake, to name just a few – but I have always felt that my books have much more in common with each other than those critics would have me believe, that there are certain identifiable preoccupations, in other words, and sometimes, in the past, I have been lured into meditating on those preoccupations. I have usually regretted it. I agree with Werner Herzog when he says, 'I don't care about themes, I care about stories'. It's not my job to know what I'm doing – at least, not at the time. It's my job to go as deep as I can. To try and give a shape to whatever I come up with. Self-consciousness is a straightjacket. Too great an awareness of precedent or meaning might hamper the writing, or even stifle it altogether. You have to write as if *nothing has been written before*. Was it Pushkin who said that every poet has to be a little bit stupid? He was talking about a kind of innocence, the innocence without which it is hard to embark on anything at all. It is a childish quality, perhaps, but then again there is nothing to match the conviction and freshness of a child's vision of the world.

'Risk and Innovation'
Rupert Thomson's Unsettling Forms

Rebecca Pohl and Christopher Vardy

Rupert Thomson is the author of ten novels and the memoir *This Party's Got to Stop*. Not only are his books numerous and highly varied, they also span nearly three decades of contemporary British writing: his debut novel, *Dreams of Leaving*, was published in 1987, his most recent novel, *Katherine Carlyle*, in 2015. One of the hallmarks of Thomson's writing is the way it ranges across genres, deploying recognizable tropes and then persistently troubling those instances of familiarity. His writing engages in distinctive ways with many concerns and critical frameworks that have been of longstanding interest to scholars of contemporary literature and culture: the essays collected in the present volume cover the topics of childhood, trauma, surveillance and history as well as gender, affect and shame. As such, Thomson's oeuvre offers a substantial corpus to investigate, both historically (in the particular span of contemporary fiction that it covers) and formally (in its movement between genres), while also touching on a number of theoretical issues that have proven central to recent work on contemporary British literature.

This collection has arisen from the first academic conference dedicated to Thomson's writing, held in Manchester in 2013. The aim of the volume is to serve as a starting point for future explorations of Thomson's work, and to elucidate some of the conversations and debate extending out of that conference. Given the range and complexity of Thomson's output, the present volume does not aspire to exhaustiveness but rather hopes to be a starting point for a growing critical discussion of his writing. As detailed in the final part of this introduction, a number of the contributions to this volume focus on Thomson's more recent work, especially *Divided Kingdom* (2005) and *Death of a Murderer* (2007). The introduction will hence discuss Thomson's earlier novels, in particular *Dreams of Leaving* (1987) and *The Five Gates of Hell* (1991), in order to complement the subsequent chapters and begin to contextualize his career. It will identify some of Thomson's key preoccupations and show how they can be traced through his oeuvre, both in the fiction and in his acclaimed memoir.

Historical contexts: the 1980s and 1990s

Thomson's writing is rarely located securely in late twentieth- or twenty-first-century Britain (much like Thomson himself, who has spent many years living in various European cities, as well as Sydney and New York). Indeed, his texts are notable for their often transnational and sometimes even spatially and temporally obscured settings. Nevertheless, his earliest work can be productively read through the contexts of its production and circulation in the late 1980s and early 1990s. Thomson's debut novel was published in 1987, a general election year which saw Margaret Thatcher re-elected for a third term in office. The 1980s have long been figured as a decisive watershed in post-war British history, the legacies of which continue to determine contemporary politics and culture (Brooker, 2010). The period saw Britain's economy restructured along neoliberal lines, with significant socio-economic costs (Harvey, 2005); it is associated with the culmination of the shift from a politics of consensus towards one of dissent or even dissensus (Waugh, 1995); leftist and radical political alternatives were increasingly fragmented, with some critics even arguing they were at an end (Fukuyama, 1992); and individual 'freedoms' were privileged over concepts of community or collectivity. Thomson's writing does not address these historical transformations in the form of obvious social realism: his hallucinatory memoir, for instance, persistently returns to the summer of 1984 and yet only briefly mentions contemporary events such as the civil disorder and state-sanctioned violence of the miners' strike. However, this is not a straightforward elision – Thomson's fiction is far from solipsistic or depoliticized. Instead, as we will see in the textual examples discussed below and in the chapters that make up this collection, the complex *political* formations of the 1980s and beyond are articulated and interrogated through oblique, de-familiarized *literary* forms.

The 1980s not only represent a political 'watershed' in British culture. They are also frequently framed as a generational shift in the literary field as now canonical writers such as Martin Amis, Salman Rushdie, Kazuo Ishiguro and Jeanette Winterson appeared on the literary stage with their landmark, and often formally experimental, social critiques. *Dreams of Leaving* was published four years after *Granta's* first 'Best of Young British Novelists' list and was accompanied by celebratory reviews remarking on 'a stunning new talent' (*Evening Standard*), with 'the talent to become a major novelist' (*The Times*). Yet despite this high praise, and the fact that Thomson was initially critically received in similar terms to 'the 1980s generation', his writing – though consistently admired and well reviewed – has not always been an easy fit with these and other generational narratives. A broad account of the recurring concerns of British literature in the late 1980s and 1990s might focus on continuities in the novels' insistent interrogation of identity politics (specifically of gender, sexuality and the nation), its preoccupation with the effects of globalization and multiculturalism, or its engagement with postmodernism and its legacies. Indeed, critical discourses in the period reflect some of these trends in their persistent concerns with pluralization and hybridity.[1] The 1990s brought with it its own particular forms of consumption and culture, from raves and tripping to the expanded mediatization of all walks of life, which resulted in an increasing artistic and literary concern with the blurring of boundaries between realities (Bentley, 2005: 1–18). The decade was also framed by two world-changing events: the fall of the Berlin Wall in 1989, which initiated the collapse of Communism and the end of the Cold War, and the 9/11 terror attacks in 2001. Cultural production in the 1990s was dominated by anxieties about history, a proliferation of cultural forms articulating and exploring trauma, as well as an increasingly hyperreal 'society of the spectacle' (Debord, 2013) being driven by rapid technological change. Thomson's early novels are representative of some of these dominant currents in literary and cultural production of the late 1980s and 1990s, and it is generative to read these texts through this historical and cultural framework. However, at the same time, and perhaps typically for Thomson, his writing unsettles neat literary and historical categorizations through its generic instability, a quality visible from his debut novel onwards.

Dreams of Leaving already gestures towards Thomson's later preoccupations with trauma and its aftermath, with departures into oddly familiar worlds and bizarre occurrences. But it is also a text of the 1980s, a text attentive to identity formation, economic inequality, different modes of capitalism, and authoritarian state power. The novel is set in two parallel worlds, one a recognizable 1980s London, the other an inexplicably isolated town called New Egypt that seems to exist outside of time. New Egypt's borders are meticulously and mercilessly controlled by a brutal police force commanded by Inspector Peach: it is a miniature, authoritarian police state whose inhabitants either try and fail to escape, reconcile themselves to a life without critical thinking, or quietly despair. The novel's protagonist, Moses Highness, is the only citizen ever to have escaped, though he has no memory of this escape, or of New Egypt, as he was an infant when his parents set him afloat in a basket. The majority of the novel is concerned with Moses's quest for his identity. Currently living off benefits in the abandoned attic of a London nightclub, Moses moves among a group of friends similarly alienated from society, and making do. Oppressiveness pervades the novel, not only in New Egypt: in London, Moses is too tall to comfortably fit anywhere; his nightclub home is called The Bunker and is routinely invaded by dodgy ruffians – its flashy owner's creditors. There is nowhere for the characters to settle, to find peace as they are constantly both on the run from and searching for their past. Indeed, Moses's whole life has felt unreal, uncanny, slightly off kilter: 'There was always that false note' (*DL*, 192).

In New Egypt, Moses's parents wither away, his father remembers his mother's 'eyes always creased at the edges by dreams of leaving' (*DL*, 121), dreams which she can never fulfil. The relation between the two worlds is unsettled when Peach, New Egypt's head of police, returns from a trip to London: 'It was almost as if the day had never happened. He was conscious of moving from a garish dream into a calm familiar reality' (*DL*, 230). To Peach, it is London that is unreal, and soon incorporated into a faint and possibly imagined memory. The parallel worlds merge at one point, further unsettling the initial logic of the text, and here the police inspector is figured as a spider waiting in his web to entrap Moses in the odd timelessness of New Egypt. The book's displaced presents offer a politicized critique of contemporary society that is neither quite speculative fiction, nor quite dystopian, but shows the two worlds precariously balanced, similarly oppressive and without much hope of solace.

There seems to be equally little prospect of escape for the protagonists of *The Five Gates of Hell*, Thomson's second novel, published in 1991. The text focuses on Jed and Nathan, tracing their occasionally intersecting lives from boyhood to late twenties as they move in and out of Moon Beach – a dystopian coastal city based around the funeral industry. This is where people go to die and to remember the dead: the poorest are cremated on an industrial scale, and the rich are buried in vast ocean cemeteries. The seemingly conventional coming-of-age narratives that structure the first chapters of *The Five Gates of Hell* barely hint at the novel's later transformation into an uncanny and nightmarish noir that is altogether more tricky to define. The novel takes on generic qualities of the thriller form in scenes where Jed works for a corrupt gangster and funeral magnate, and in the ending which ties the different strands of the plot together. This thriller narrative, however, is itself interspersed with vignettes of Nathan travelling and working as a life-guard. And a pervasive sense of the dystopian imaginary lurking behind the everyday is reinforced as the text persistently turns back toward Moon Beach:

> Sometimes he looked at the clouds and wondered what percentage ashes they were. Sometimes he wondered how many dead people

there were to a cloud. How many dead people came down with the rain. (*FGH*, 159–160)

This especially sinister line is exemplary of the novel, but it is also more broadly representative of Thomson's prose. Unsettling overtones and undertones, strongest in his earlier novels, colour much of his writing to date, where characters reel out of control after bizarre encounters. In *The Five Gates of Hell*, subjects and social relations are exposed as precarious and liable to inexplicable, violent disruption: an isolated, peaceful commune is transformed by a mysterious, aggressive newcomer; adolescents die under strange circumstances; young men vanish from the streets, murdered by a sadistic funerary oligarch. A sense of barely-averted, imminent yet often indefinable crisis is a recurrent theme of Thomson's work, and one which figures throughout the essays in this collection:

> He saw the place where he'd grown up. Somehow there was shadow even in the yellow sunlight on the lawn. As if all colour, even the brightest, held darkness. Nothing was safe. Everything could turn, give way. Fifty miles north of Moon Beach they drove into a gas station and he couldn't see anything for a moment. It was just like being in the shadow after being in the sun. But that was what it felt like to be going home. (*FGH*, 12)

Critical contexts: unsettling genres

One of the distinctive features of Thomson's writing is the way it experiments with genre, both within and across texts. The characteristic generic instability of his output, which can be traced back to his own conflicted stance towards literature as both a moral imperative and income-generating profession (Holmes, 2014), speaks to the contemporary cultural interest in questions of genre. While genre is central to the marketing of literature (Squires, 2007), it is a complex term that operates as both a marketing tool and an aesthetic value. Critics such as Robert Eaglestone have identified genre as a key category for analyses of contemporary literary production. Eaglestone (2013: 26–36) shows how genre structures debates about literary value as well as the concept of literature itself with the newly introduced category of 'literary fiction'. More recently, Val McDermid caused controversy with her remarks about the politics of genre when she stated:

> [The crime novel is] critical of the status quo [...] It often gives voice to characters who are not comfortably established in the world – immigrants, sex workers, the poor, the old. The dispossessed and the people who don't vote. The thriller, on the other hand, tends towards the conservative, probably because the threat implicit in the thriller is the world turned upside down. (McDermid, 2015)

The strong reactions to these comments shows that genre as a term carries critical weight both within the academy and in wider cultural debates when it comes to the attribution of literary value (Freedland, 2015).

Genre can be thought as a way of distinguishing different types of text or narrative; it is central to the commissioning, marketing and selling of fiction, and it is a key way of thinking through literary influence: where a text comes from and what concepts or tropes from the past are being recycled, reworked, or departed from. Genres are ways of mapping historical trajectories but are also always in the process of being transformed. As Middleton and Woods (2000: 7–8) suggest, '[l]ike language, [genre] exists only as it is practiced, and its codes are no more than partially articulated recognitions of its more sedimented forms'. This recognition is crucial to genre's operations, though, and it is here that Thomson's novels offer fruitful ground for analysis. The generic instability, especially across the range of his oeuvre, only becomes meaningful as such because instances of genre have been recognized. The simultaneous invoking and undercutting of particular generic tropes is what makes genre such an important and curious category for approaching his work, and vice versa.

Some brief examples will help to illustrate this. There are, for instance, identifiably historical forms amongst Thomson's novels. In 2013 Thomson published a historical novel set in seventeenth-century Florence. *Secrecy* tells the story of Gaetano Zummo, a Sicilian wax artist famed for his 'plague pieces', who becomes the Tuscan Grand Duke's personal court artist, tasked with crafting a perfect female model. Embedded in the wax figure he creates is an invisible foetus, an image that recurs throughout the novel: his secret lover Faustina bears him a daughter he will never know; and Faustina herself, as the final turns of plot reveal, is the Grand Duke's wife's secret illegitimate child. The characters are based on historical persons and the novel is replete with temporal, physical and procedural detail that implies accuracy under the guise of a realist mode:

> Covering two lengths of string in pig fat, I fixed them to the girl's left leg, one on either side, so they stretched all the way from her hip to her ankle, then I reached for the sack of powdered gypsum and heaped several scoops into a bowl. When casting Fiore's hands, I had used lukewarm water, and the plaster had set too rapidly. This time I would use cold water and a sprinkling of grog – a pulverized burnt clay – which would slow down the chemical reaction and give me a little more control. (*S*, 145)

However, as Adam Mars-Jones argues in his review of *Secrecy*, this insistence on precision can be read as part of Thomson's 'unpicking and reweaving' of the genre, an exaggeration of generic conventions that troubles the claim to realism echoing throughout the conventional historical novel (Mars-Jones, 2013). This insistence is also discernible in an earlier novel, *Air and Fire* (1993), which itself brims with precise historical detail:

> All the longitudinal elements are now laid out on site in the usual manner, along with the majority of the end posts and tie bars, and I find myself marvelling once again at the intrinsic simplicity of the system 1 B2 4, 5 B4 8, etc. upon which all our endeavours are based. We have employed dry foundations, sinking to just half a metre; given the quality of the subsoil in El Pueblo and the nature of the searing forces in this particular structure, there seemed no necessity to ensure against unequal settling. (*AF*, 71)

This text, too, unsettles as much as it enacts the genre of historical fiction. The novel is firmly rooted in its nineteenth-century setting, and again the historical dimension is foregrounded through accuracy of reference and descriptive detail: the passage relates at length the unloading of the steel elements which are to be assembled into a church designed by Gustave Eiffel. It is written by one of Eiffel's protégés, Théo. The 'simple system' is rendered oblique by the reference to the serial numbers of the elements, emphasizing the discrete elements that do not yet, and never will, come together into a meaningful whole. The description seems abstract precisely because of its excessive specificity which is indecipherable to the reader of the novel who does not know what 'B2' refers to, or how it fits into a meaningful system. The shorthand 'in the usual manner' makes sense for two experts communicating with each other, but holds little information for the reader – except in as much as it locates the letter firmly in a historically specific moment. Similarly, the geological and geographical detail in the letter invokes the mode of realism and yet its descriptiveness is purely technical, it does not invoke the landscape. This particular moment of historical detail is taken from a letter within the novel, which is by turns epistolary, hallucinatory and historical as it tracks a French expatriate couple's attempts to live in a secluded nineteenth-century Mexican desert village. And it is precisely in this emphasis on detail, which is systematically undercut by unreliable narration, lack of communication and comprehension between characters and the mirages and absurdities of life in a secluded desert village, that Thomson 'unpicks' the genre once more.

In contrast, Thomson's novel *Death of a Murderer* (2007) is striking in its lack of precise detail despite its clear historical reference point. It explores the obsessive cultural production of selective stories about the past, but always through the murky, fragile prism of individual memory. It is certainly a *kind* of historical fiction, but there is no historical 'setting' or easily locatable 'past'. The novel takes place in a hospital morgue following the death of 'Moors Murderess' Myra Hindley, though the name and 'real' identity of the body guarded by policeman Billy are suggestively occluded throughout. In many ways, this is an unconventionally historical novel that reassembles the history it references through complex associations and characters' memories rather than exploring historical events through the kind of stable temporal setting that most often defines the realist mode. The significance of *Death of a Murderer*'s unusual modes of recollection and historical narrative are explored in greater depth in two dedicated chapters in this volume (Vardy, Gordon). Though in many ways a historical novel, *Secrecy* could equally be classed as a thriller. Waiting for his nemesis, Stufa, at the close of the framed narrative, Zummo's tense anticipation, buffered by the blankets of oppressive snow, is carefully crafted:

> The day passed in fits and starts. Time behaved like the rabbit. Leaping forwards, standing still.
> I went downstairs and stoked the fire. I tried to eat. I listened.
> He didn't come.
> I found it difficult to imagine what might be keeping him. Perhaps, as in a legend, he had fallen into a sleep that would last for centuries. Perhaps I would die waiting. Become another ghost.
> This house, this snow.
> This loneliness. (*S*, 288)

Stuck in a derelict house in the middle of the woods, Zummo has no option but to sit still and wait, not unlike a rabbit in headlights as it freezes – before haring off. Time is no longer felt as measurable, it is all duration and no passing and it is no longer stable but jumps and starts, adding to the sense of oppression as well as signifying Zummo's precarious grasp on the situation: instruments of reason such as time-keeping have become meaningless. As Zummo obsesses about Stufa, the cleric becomes an absent presence casting his looming shadow over the house and its temporary inhabitant. The repetition of the demonstrative pronoun 'this' in relation to concepts previously undeclared reinforces the sense of duration as it releases them from specificity. When Stufa finally does arrive at the house, torture instruments clinking and chanting his revised version of Luke 1:46 into the snowy silence, heard but not seen by character and reader alike, the tension is palpable.

The eponymous narrator of Thomson's latest novel, *Katherine Carlyle* (2015), is simultaneously in search of a stable genre as well as a coherent origin narrative. As she runs northwards across Europe, certain neither of what she is running from nor what she is running towards, she reflects, '[t]his isn't a detective story. Do I want it to be?'

(*KC*, 112). Her journey takes her from Rome to Berlin to Moscow and finally to the Svalbard peninsula on the Arctic Circle. Taken together with the novel's epigraph from Mary Shelley's *Frankenstein*, this Arctic trajectory insists on intertextual parallels: the quest for origin, the unstable definition of the human. An IVF baby, as an embryo Katherine was frozen for eight years before implantation, a fact that continues to determine her life: 'there is a memory of that time. I *carry* it. Not in my brain necessarily – not *consciously* – but in my bones. My marrow' (*KC*, 141). Like the monster in *Frankenstein*, Katherine is struggling at the intersection of embodied life and artifice, a struggle that is framed by her stalled, frozen origin and the frozenness of the barren Svalbard landscape she attaches herself to. This landscape is not only frozen, it is also empty and lies in 'absolute' darkness (*KC*, 230), echoing the wild, remote and empty landscapes of much gothic fiction, and specifically the packed ice across which Frankenstein's monster makes his last desperate attempt to escape. Gothic tropes abound in the novel, from deserted landscapes and the persistent spectre of sexual violence, to suggestive ghostly visitations:

> I have the sudden conviction that somebody else is in the pool. When I turn at the deep end and peer ahead of me there's no one there, just a wide shifting box of green-brown water. I struggle to explain the rush of apprehension and euphoria. As I keep swimming up and down, the sense that I'm not alone intensifies, becomes specific. There are people in either side of me, and slightly behind me, just out of range of my field of vision. The pool is empty. But as I swim back towards the deep end I have the feeling once again that I'm accompanied. We're in a loose V-shape, like geese flying south for the winter. A shiver ripples through me. (*KC*, 260)

And yet, these tropes and intertextual associations do not quite assemble into the shape of a gothic novel.

Reading Thomson's texts through the categories of the historical novel, the thriller or the gothic – and we can also include the kinds of dystopian writing discussed in the first part of this introduction – highlights productive patterns and intersections within this eclectic body of work. Yet it becomes clear even from the preceding overview

11

that his writing also frustrates the imposition of stable definitions of genre. Thomson's novels (and his memoir too, with its meditation on modes of writing and remembering) often fuse different genres and forms into hybrid, idiosyncratic narratives that toy with and veer away from expectations about what particular kinds of writing 'do': how they function, how they develop and how they end. Even *Secrecy*, whose realist mode, use of the 'necessary anachronism' (Lukacs, 1962) and quasi-postmodern framing device (Hutcheon, 1989) conform to definitions of the historical novel, and *Divided Kingdom*, which is the closest Thomson has come to writing a recognizably 'dystopian fiction', subvert and challenge these categories and trajectories at the same time as they operate within them. The perceived disparity in his oeuvre is then, perhaps, one of the things that characterizes it.

Thomson's writing exceeds, resists and unsettles taxonomies or neat categorization. It contains many of the key conceptual and critical currents in contemporary fiction: trauma narratives, literatures of memory, historical fictions, thrillers, noir, dystopian tropes and forms, interrogations of the relationship between the global and the local. There are intersections and patterns but no 'macro-novel' here in the sense that David Mitchell has proposed for his own writing (Mason, 2010). There is experimentation, but no unifying experimental aesthetic and no generic trajectory to impose in retrospect. Thomson 'creatively mix[es] genres and traditions' (Eaglestone, 2013: 33), and the generic instability of Thomson's writing is cumulative. In many ways, Thomson's oeuvre functions as a metaphor for contemporary fiction in the wake of 'high' postmodernism in the 1980s and 1990s: its many displaced currents and crossovers; its artistic and generic diversity without (and without any need for the imposition of) one dominant concept or form. Fixing contemporary literary texts as exemplars of (or deviations from) a particular critical taxonomy, or analysing them within a single overarching historical genealogy or theoretical school, risks smoothing over their contradictions and ambivalences and eliding the compelling interpretive difficulty of textuality. Reading and writing about Thomson's work through the prism of genres highlights both the generative qualities and the limitations of these ever-changing categories.

Structure of this book

Where this introduction has offered a historical contextualization of Thomson's writing, and has begun to consider his early novels through the lens of contemporary literary analysis, in particular concepts of genre, the subsequent chapters locate Thomson's writing in critical debate through a variety of theoretical approaches. As discussed in relation to both *Dreams of Leaving* and *The Five Gates of Hell*, spatial politics and identity are crucial concerns in Thomson's texts. Robert Duggan's chapter explores these politics in greater depth through a case study of *Divided Kingdom*. Duggan is particularly interested in the figure of the border and its attendant processes of inclusion and exclusion. Though essentially interned in his quarter of the divided kingdom, the novel's protagonist will end up crossing between all four quarters. In so doing, he sacrifices the sense of security promised by the clear identity he has been allocated by the authorities and becomes instead a floating signifier as he chases his originary trauma across the country. Duggan's investigation of the ways in which security is both a spatial effect and bound up with a sense of belonging is informed by the work of two key French theorists of spatial practices, Michel de Certeau and Gaston Bachelard. The chapter is interested in the interlinked instability of space, identity and genre as it plays out in the novel, but also in the ways in which it can be situated within a tradition of literary texts concerned with similar processes.

Iain Robinson's chapter also focuses on *Divided Kingdom* and complements Duggan's reading of identity as it relates to security and belonging by developing a discussion of identity in relation to dislocation. The chapter shows how the spatial borders parallel the ruptures in the main character's identity, and how crossing these external and internal boundaries represents an attempt to work through his trauma. Robinson's key critical point of reference is Michel Foucault's writing on discipline and power which, like de Certeau's work, offers an analysis of the power politics of social practices. Both theorists are interested in the way power operates spatially and as both Duggan and Robinson demonstrate, Thomson's novel asks similar questions. Robinson's reading is informed by critical work on psycho-geography which begins to trouble the power dynamic set up by Foucault and de Certeau. In particular, he looks at the ways in which psycho-geography privileges the subconscious as a strategy for encountering and resisting spatial politics. Robinson goes on to show how Thomson's novel responds to and develops a long tradition of dystopian fiction, suggesting that the play of power relations in the book is figured through haunting and spectrality. These recurrent dynamics in Thomson's oeuvre bear similarities with the concerns of other contemporary writers working in or with the dystopian tradition.

Christopher Vardy's chapter investigates *Death of a Murderer*, arguing that through its presentation of child abuse the novel interrogates constitutive cultural narratives of childhood. The novel reveals the pervasive contemporary nostalgia for childhood in the recent past to be illusory and damaging. Idyllic, pre-lapsarian narratives are exposed as serving adult desires and doing little justice to either the complexities of the past or historical experiences of children. Crucially, the text also destabilizes the widespread understanding of 'the child' as an uncomplicated, 'natural' embodiment of progress, possibility and futurity. This is figured not only through the murder and abuse that leaves children forever 'lost in time', but also through the many other children who punctuate the text and are trapped in unstable lives, or face uncertain futures. In *Death of a Murderer*, childhood and abuse become anxious contemporary metaphors for both the determining power of the past and the fear of a precarious, hopeless future.

Rhona Gordon's chapter picks up on the theme of haunting to show how *Death of a Murderer* explores the complex operations of contemporary cultural memory in relation to recent historical events and analyses the often unreliable and always politicized ways in which personal and collective memory interact with one another. The novel's protagonist is not only haunted by the spectre of Myra Hindley as he stands guard over her corpse – he is also profoundly disturbed by the 'ordinariness' of that spectre. Gordon's chapter thinks about the banality of evil and the reductive moralism of good and bad.

While similarly interested in this undercurrent of abuse that appears throughout Thomson's writing, Kaye Mitchell's chapter shifts the critical focus from trauma and memory to an analysis of affect.

Affect theory has gained substantial purchase in recent critical discourse, not least as a methodological response to trauma, and Mitchell shows how Thomson's work speaks to this critical tradition from Sylvan Tomkins onwards. Affect is here seen as a fundamental component of identity formation, and crucially, of re-formation. The particular affect Mitchell focuses on is shame, a key concern of recent debates in queer theory and gender studies. Hence, while she, too, shows how a Thomson character's identity is dismantled by trauma, her specific concern is with the gendering of that identity, with the relation between shame and masculinity. Her chapter shows how Thomson's novel *The Book of Revelation* centres on the production of gendered shame. Mitchell places this focus in a wider literary and theoretical context, tracing the default gendering of shame in critical discourse and concludes that although *The Book of Revelation* appears to trouble a cultural commonplace in which shame is feminized, the novel cannot quite sustain the critique it mounts. Nevertheless, Mitchell argues, Thomson's novel offers an important and distinctive starting point for such considerations.

Rebecca Pohl returns to the earlier discussions of space, but her analysis is distinct from the earlier approaches in the way it thinks space in relation to affect. Beginning from a wider view of Thomson's oeuvre, Pohl looks to engage with the category of 'atmosphere' in order to analyse the potential for continuity across Thomson's writing with a specific focus on *The Insult*. Atmosphere is a slippery term which nonetheless seems appropriate, Pohl argues, to think through the unsettling regularities in these otherwise very various texts. The chapter outlines something of the history and the difficulty of the idea of atmosphere, indicating the ways in which it has recently begun to be recuperated in literary and cultural analysis (sometimes in the guise of 'mood'), and especially in German scholarship where the famously untranslatable *Stimmung* has never quite lost purchase. Crucially, Pohl links space and affect in this analysis: her reading of Thomson's novel is both a specific attempt at thinking through his disparate oeuvre as a whole, and a specific example of what it means to analyse atmosphere.

The final chapter by John McAuliffe returns the volume full circle to Thomson's earliest novels, via his memoir of 2010, as well as concluding the collection with a poet's view on the oeuvre. McAuliffe's central question asks what it means to (re)read an author's literary output in light of their autobiographical writing. In doing so, he revisits a number of debates introduced by earlier chapters, such as the workings of memory and questions of shame. The chapter situates Thomson in a clear tradition of fiction writers going on to produce memoirs, and draws out the connections to Thomson's debut novel in a way reminiscent of critical responses to Jeanette Winterson's 2011 memoir *Why Be Happy When You Could Be Normal?* McAuliffe's chapter not only demonstrates how Thomson's memoir firmly places him in contemporary literary fictional developments, but also opens into the field of poetry, and more specifically ekphrasis; he shows how Thomson's later writings adopt and develop this ancient literary form and tradition.

Taken together, the chapters in this collection demonstrate the many ways in which Thomson's writing focuses key critical debates in the contemporary literary field, including discussions of genre, gender, trauma, affect and life writing. They share a perception that his texts do not sit easily with any one or the other of these areas of concern, that they are curiously unassimilable to a programme or a particular problem; that they tend, as Mitchell's essay suggests, even to cede the authoritative position of critique. This volume is intended to lay the groundwork for further debate and analysis of Thomson's writing, one of the most consistently innovative and unsettling bodies of work in contemporary fiction.

Acknowledgements

The title of this chapter is a quotation from Rupert Thomson, Interview, *Huffington Post*, 18 September 2014.

Note

1 On hybridity in the context of postcolonial theory, e.g. Homi Bhabha, *The Location of Culture* (1994). In the context of gender theory, e.g. Donna

Haraway (1991). In the context of cultural studies e.g. Stuart Hall et al. (1992). For a critique see Robert Young (1995). On plurality, e.g. Fredric Jameson (1992).

Works cited

Bentley, Nick (2005) *British Fiction of the 1990s*. London: Routledge.

Bhabha, Homi (1994) *The Location of Culture*. Abingdon: Routledge.

Brooker, Joe (2010) *Literature of the 1980s: After the Watershed*. Edinburgh: Edinburgh University Press.

Debord, Guy (2013) *The Society of the Spectacle*, trans. Black & Red. London: Notting Hill.

Eaglestone, Robert (2013) *Contemporary Fiction: A Very Short Introduction*. Oxford: Oxford University Press.

Freedland, Jonathan (2015) 'Thrillers are politically conservative? That's not right', *Guardian*, 3 April, URL (consulted August 2015): http://www.theguardian.com/books/booksblog/2015/apr/03/thrillers-politically-conservative-val-mcdermid-crime-fiction-jonathan-freedland

Fukuyama, Francis (1992) *The End of History and the Last Man*. London: Hamish Hamilton.

Hall, Stuart, David Held and Tony McGrew (eds) (1992) *Modernity and Its Futures*. Cambridge: Polity.

Haraway, Donna (1991) 'A Cyborg Manifesto: Science, Technology and Socialist-Feminism in the Late Twentieth Century', in *Simians, Cyborgs and Women: The Reinvention of Nature*, pp. 149–81. Abingdon: Routledge.

Harvey, David (2005) *A Brief History of Neoliberalism*. Oxford: Oxford University Press.

Holmes, Jason (2014) 'Rupert Thomson Interview: "To Write Fiction at All Is a Moral Act"', *The Huffington Post*, 18 September, URL (consulted April 2015): http://www.huffingtonpost.co.uk/jason-holmes/rupert-thomson-interview-_b_5837914.html

Hutcheon, Linda (1989) *The Politics of Postmodernism*. London: Routledge.

Jameson, Fredric (1992) *Postmodernism, Or the Logic of Late Capitalism*. London: Verso.

Lukács, Georg (1962) *The Historical Novel*, trans. Hannah Mitchell and Stanley Mitchell. Boston, MA: Beacon Press.

Mars-Jones, Adam (2013) 'The screams were silver', *London Review of Books* 35(8): 19–20.

Mason, Wyatt (2010) 'David Mitchell, the Experimentalist', *The New York Times Magazine*, 25 June, URL (consulted April 2015): http://www.nytimes.com/2010/06/27/magazine/27mitchell-t.html

McDermid, Val (2015) 'Why crime fiction is leftwing and thrillers are rightwing', *Guardian*, 1 April, URL (consulted April 2015): http://www.theguardian.com/books/booksblog/2015/apr/01/why-crime-fiction-is-leftwing-and-thrillers-are-rightwing

Middleton, Peter and Tim Woods (2000) *Literatures of Memory: History, Time and Space in Postwar Writing*. Manchester: Manchester University Press.

Squires, Claire (2007) *Marketing Literature: The Making of Contemporary Writing in Britain*. Basingstoke: Palgrave Macmillan.

Waugh, Patricia (1995) *Harvest of the Sixties: English Literature and its Background, 1960–1990*. Oxford: Oxford University Press.

Young, Robert (1995) *Colonial Desire: Hybridity in Theory, Culture and Race*. London: Routledge.

'Border Games' and Security in the Work of Rupert Thomson

Robert Duggan

The extent to which Rupert Thomson's fiction engages creatively with space and place seems at times difficult to overstate, from the mysterious southern English town of New Egypt in *Dreams of Leaving* (1987), the inhabitants of which are not permitted to leave, to the unnamed and obliquely glimpsed European urban spaces of *The Insult* (1996). In particular, his works frequently delve into how an individual negotiates the borders of particular spaces, the fiction staging circulation within as well as moves across established boundaries. The Thomson novel that I will explore below, *Divided Kingdom* (2005), can be read as a crystallization, in a more clearly structured and abstract form, of this key preoccupation with borders and leaving that is prominent at so many points within Thomson's oeuvre. A perhaps ambiguous journey away from security underlies many of Thomson's novels and this chapter will examine how far *Divided Kingdom*'s narrative of border crossing and in-between states intersects with concerns around family and belonging, and ultimately plays a fundamental role in his artistic enterprise as a writer. Thomson persistently plays with readers' expectations and expands the possibilities of contemporary fiction, and this chapter will show how he draws on a variety of literary, historical and artistic influences to create an intriguing and moving account of the search for identity and a future in a challenging world.

Growing up in *Divided Kingdom*

In *Divided Kingdom* the UK has been divided into four zones according to the medieval theory of humours, with people confined or forcibly transported to one of the four quarters of the country. A person's sanguine, choleric, phlegmatic or melancholic humour defines their place in one of the four territories, each of which is associated with one of the four elements and named according to the colour associated with the respective humour: Red for sanguine, Yellow for choleric, Blue for phlegmatic, Green for melancholic. Travel between the zones is strictly controlled, with patrolled borders between them, and diplomatic missions and deportations comprise the principal traffic. Each zone is defined by its humour and supposedly inhabited only by those of the matching humour, with the various cultures and lifestyles in each zone reflecting their different 'nature'. The book's front endpaper has a colour-coded map that follows the geographical outline of Britain and Northern Ireland, identifying the divisions between the four zones, whose respective capitals have been carved out of a divided city located on the map roughly where one would expect to find London. The transition from the United Kingdom to this current divided one is known as the Rearrangement, a euphemistic term that conceals the traumatic nature of the experience of relocation that the novel will go on to explore. The narrative promulgated by the four new governments, however, is that the Rearrangement was both necessary and successful, and is the final solution to decades of increasing unhappiness and social turmoil:

> For decades, if not for centuries, the country had employed a complicated web of manners and convention to draw a veil over its true nature, but now, finally, it had thrown off all pretence to be anything other than it was – northern, inward-looking, fundamentally barbaric. (*DK*, 8)

The rhetorical assertion that the Rearrangement effected the revelation of an underlying 'natural' truth about the country and its peoples is a feature of this political discourse and the novel explores how far such a belief is sincerely held, by the public at large and by those who administer their affairs.

The narrator of *Divided Kingdom* is aged eight or nine when he is taken from his biological family and moved to a holding station named Thorpe Hall. After some time being schooled here, he is given the new name of Thomas Parry and subsequently transferred to the Sanguine Quarter and a new adoptive family in the first section of the book. The boy's memory in the opening scene of the novel is of his mother calling his name as he is taken away, but it is not until page 47 that the reader learns that his original name was Matthew Micklewright. The protagonist grows up in the household of Victor Parry and his daughter Marie in the Sanguine Quarter and learns to hide his pain at his lost family and to satisfy officials that he temperamentally conforms to his new community. He later discovers that these attempts are matched by his adoptive relatives' surreptitious and potentially dangerous acts of remembering the mother in the family, who was forcibly transferred to the Yellow Quarter, a choleric place where the chaotic violence of the residents is matched by brutal official curfews. Thomas's ability to connect with his adoptive family's pain however is hampered by his circumstances and personal history:

> In truth, I wasn't all that curious. I was just trying to fit in. The events that had upset Victor seemed academic to me, remote, even foreign. Perhaps I lacked the proper context ... or perhaps it was the eerie matter-of-factness of a child who, having experienced a trauma of his own, decides simply to get on with the business of living, which in my case meant acquainting myself with my new environment. (*DK*, 24)

The deceptively simple-sounding task of 'the business of living' becomes the novel's central preoccupation, one shaped by traumatic separation. In this, *Divided Kingdom* shares with other Thomson books such as *The Insult* and *The Book of Revelation* (1999) the reverberations and consequences of injury, imprisonment, abuse and forced exile on protagonists seeking and often struggling to understand the foreign-seeming world around them and to find a (secure) place within it.

These household secrets are Thomas's earliest inklings of the discontinuities that permeate the divided kingdom, discontinuities that are both the worrying sign of a chaotic social schema full of pitfalls and, Thomas gradually learns, gaps or inconsistencies in the system with the potential to be exploited. While a student at university he is approached by a member of staff from the innocuous-sounding Ministry of Health and Social Security and informed by her that, 'We've been watching you' (*DK*, 59). What ensues is the offer of a government job, but the ominous remark evokes the ambivalent quality of the surveillance as a nurturing process supporting growth on the one hand and as an oppressive intrusion into privacy and personal liberty on the other. The novel repeatedly investigates this double-edged quality of security and borders, as a protective armature necessary for personal development, and as imprisoning structures that curb freedom and distort relationships. Parry takes a job in the government service and on a foreign trip to Aquaville, the capital city of the phlegmatics in the Blue Quarter, goes to an enigmatic club called the Bathysphere, where he has a strange immersive experience of being in his original bedroom with his mother downstairs calling his name. This experience encourages Parry to wonder about the fate of his mother and he begins a journey around the different zones, each of which has its distinctive atmosphere and way of life, which makes up the main body of the novel.

Parry's childhood in the Red Quarter, the home of sanguine people, is an ostensibly tranquil one in a zone marked by equanimity and harmony, a kind of petit-bourgeois contentment, without much in the way of either danger or excitement. One of Parry's teachers at Thorpe Hall quotes to the class from Thomas Walkington's early seventeenth-century treatise *The Optick Glass of Humours* on the superiority of the 'sanguine complection' over other humours (*DK*, 13), and it is clear that the residents of the Red Quarter are encouraged to regard themselves as the luckiest people in the divided kingdom. Mary Floyd-Wilson in *English Ethnicity and Race in Early Modern Drama* (2003) argues that this privileging of the sanguine is part of Renaissance 'geohumoralism' (Floyd-Wilson, 2003: 39) whereby different humours are ascribed to different parts of the world, and so Walkington is offering a specifically *English* take on the relative merits of the humour commonly attributed in the period to English people. By extension, the provincial peacefulness and apparent social harmony of Parry's childhood in the Red Quarter has a quintessentially English flavour, and Parry is struck by how the drycleaner Mr Page looks as though he's always smiling (*DK*, 27) and how the political leader Michael Song looks 'almost literally *polished*, and how convivial too, like some worldly uncle you wished you saw more often' (*DK*, 37). There are however hints that other, less appealing, aspects of Englishness lie just beyond the quarter's borders.

Part of the atmosphere of the Red Quarter is an aversion to risk, and early on in the novel we learn that '[t]o sanguine people, motorways signified aggression, rage, fatigue, monotony and death. Motorways were choleric, in other words, and had no place in the Red Quarter' (*DK*, 36). Soon after moving in with his new family, Parry meets a former Thorpe Hall school friend, Bracewell, and together they explore the borders of their town:

> We must have absorbed some of the atmosphere of the times, I suppose, since we invented a whole series of what we referred to privately as 'border games'. One morning we cycled further north than usual and found a section of the motorway that was in the process of being dug up. In our minds, the area instantly became a no-man's land, with construction workers standing in for guards. (*DK*, 40)

The border games of Parry and Bracewell require them to take turns playing the roles of fugitive and guard, one patrolling while the other tries to cross the road without being seen. The games prefigure Parry's later journeys between the zones, early on in the novel as a government official conducting the forcible transfer of a young woman to the Yellow Quarter, and then later as a clandestine traveller attempting to avoid detection when crossing the border, and blend in with the local people. This no-man's land, the empty area between zones, becomes a site of great significance in the novel and Parry will spend much of the book testing the boundaries of the divided kingdom, both in terms of geographical borders and the more speculative differences between people. The narrator's reflections on having 'absorbed some of the atmosphere of the times' also point along a different (geographical) axis toward absorbing some of the 'spirit of the place', and Thomson's narrative registers the effects of both spatial and temporal influences on his vulnerable but adventurous protagonist. The narrative suggests that through the authorities' systems of segregation, forced adoption and strict social regulation, the 'character' or 'humour' of each zone can become a self-sustaining force shaping the inhabitants' lives. This leads to the question of how far the Rearrangement codifies existing differences between people and how far it constructs and enforces them.

Jean Rhys and no-man's land

The significance of no-man's land is heralded by *Divided Kingdom*'s epigraph from Jean Rhys, a paratextual invocation existing on the margins of Thomson's text. Rhys was deeply concerned with no-man's land, and her work marks a complex engagement with Britain, existing both inside and outside its borders. Her often challenging experiences as a white West Indian living in Europe form a background to her fiction's frequently distressing accounts of migrant life and feelings of non-belonging. Her most famous work, *Wide Sargasso Sea* (1997, first published 1966), takes its title from an in-between place that is not a place, an empty zone of the Atlantic where ships were often becalmed, stranded between the Caribbean and Britain. This most famous of liminal spaces was anticipated in earlier books by Rhys, from *Good Morning Midnight* (2000, first published 1939) which begins in a dead-end street or *impasse* in Paris, to the opening lines of *Voyage in the Dark* (1969, first published 1934), the first sentence of which is Thomson's epigraph:

> It was as if a curtain had fallen, hiding everything I had ever known. It was almost like being born again. The colours were different, the smells different, the feeling things gave you right down inside yourself was different ... Sometimes it was as if I were back there and as if England were a dream. At other times England was the real thing and

out there was the dream, but I could never fit them together. (Rhys, 1969: 7)

This dramatic transition between places creates a great confusion in Rhys's protagonist Anna Morgan's mind: where does she belong, which place is real? And the quote anticipates 'Rochester' arguing with Antoinette in *Wide Sargasso Sea* over whether England or the West Indies is more real.[1] A cognitive gap opens up between the two 'realities' that cannot 'fit ... together'. One of the defining experiences of reading *Divided Kingdom*, and other work by Thomson, is precisely this feeling of disorientation, where the experience of geographical dislocation creates an inward turn and is the catalyst for the line between dreams and reality becoming blurred. The altered UK explored by Parry occupies a liminal position between dream and reality, and the reader experiences the places he visits as at once familiar and deeply strange. The difficulty of mentally reconciling two apparently separate and possibly opposed realities, and the loss of stable reference points that Rhys repeatedly presents in her novels, are part of Parry's predicament as he navigates the divided kingdom on his own voyage in the dark.

Parry and his female friend Odell's experience on the streets of a northern town in the Yellow Quarter on the day of a football match embodies *Divided Kingdom*'s distinctive mixture of the foreign with the (to some British readers, at least) alarmingly recognizable aspects of life in the UK:

> We ducked into a doorway as a second group of men swayed towards us. They were singing strange savage songs that I'd never heard before. With their cropped hair and their hard, exultant faces, they seemed to have sealed themselves off from the rest of us. It was like the divided kingdom in miniature – the same tribalism, the same deep need to belong. (*DK*, 346)

Thomson creates a vivid impression of football tribalism, the massed ranks of police in body armour, the savage chanting, broken shop windows, the rioting on the terraces, the fighting on the pitch, the helicopter with its searchlight, to show how a nominal leisure activity can resemble and perhaps even foment mass disorder and social breakdown. This recognizable part of everyday life in the Yellow Quarter (and lamentably, occasionally in the real UK) is not some sort of resistance, but on the contrary the distillation of the logic of segregation into a more concentrated form. The energy which fuels such tribal shows of aggression, and which satisfies the 'deep need to belong', also keeps the kingdom and its peoples divided. Parry's series of displacements and successive experiences of expatriation force him to reflect on how far he, too, is motivated by a need to belong, despite witnessing the ugliness of tribalism as part of his defining experiences of non-belonging in places and communities that can so often be cruel to anyone who does not fit in.

Divided Kingdom pays particular attention to the reproduction of these tribal attitudes in children, not only in the account of Parry's upbringing but in the scenes in which children participate in the activities of their elders. On the day after the football match (the result of which Parry never discovers) a gang of children 'some as young as five or six' (*DK*, 352) attempt to rob Parry, and he is 'aware of the smallness of the hands that pushed and pulled at' him (*DK*, 353). It is only after his companion Odell uses an aerosol against the children that a shaken Parry manages to escape with his possessions. Before reaching the Yellow Quarter city Parry and Odell had entered a village where some kind of festivity was taking place:

> A crowd had gathered there, beneath a large, gnarled oak, and once the racket the van was making had died away I could hear the shrieks and squeals of children. There must be an attraction of some kind, I thought. A juggler, perhaps. A puppet show. (*DK*, 339)

It is only after he has left the village that he learns the 'attraction' was the public display of the mutilated heads of strangers for the entertainment of local people who have 'eyes like bits of wet glass' (*DK*, 340). The aggression that pervades the Yellow Quarter, 'a sour embittered place, a place that had turned its fury against itself' (*DK*, 340), seems to permeate every aspect of its residents' lives, whether they are young or old, and Parry himself is not immune to the pervasive atmosphere of aggression:

By the time we reached our first village, something unexpected had occurred. My mood had soured. I was in a bad temper after all, a genuine bad temper, which meant I no longer had to worry about standing out. (*DK*, 338)

The reader is left to wonder how far his displays of anger and belligerence are merely a simulation to protect himself and how far they are intrinsic to his personality, only awaiting the right environment in which to emerge.

As so often in Thomson's fiction, including the arrival of Zummo in Renaissance Florence in Thomson's recent novel *Secrecy* (2013), foregoing or being deprived of the security of the familiar necessitates one's immersion in a potentially dangerous 'foreign element'. The emphasis on immersion in *Divided Kingdom* is very noticeable, and there is a high degree of congruence between the main character's experience of his journey across the zones and the reader's literary experience of immersion in strange, but strangely familiar, places and situations. Like entering a bathysphere or diving-bell, the reader becomes immersed in this semi-recognizable country, its customs and ways of life and the journey has both geographical and psychic dimensions. In a sense, the bathysphere's protective skin is something that Parry will have to forsake if he is to encounter directly what lies outside, and his journey to the different zones brings out different aspects of his personality as he is shaped by the different places he visits. This is very different to being a voyeur, safely watching from inside the diving-bell, in that both protagonist and reader are subjected to this sometimes threatening dislocation, taken out of their comfort zone, and compelled to feel their way through foreign territory. When toward the end of the book Parry has visited all four quarters, he becomes one of the White People, itinerants who, due to apparent mental impairment, exist outside the system of humours and so wander across borders. Significantly, Parry does not simply simulate being one of the White People, he actually becomes one, fully immerses himself, loses his power of speech and is alternately ignored and victimized by the choleric people of the Yellow Quarter. An achromatic, as they are officially designated, is a kind of legal nonperson 'lost in a pocket of history' (*DK*, 125), with no place in the new divided kingdom. Without the colour and status that guarantees legal identity, they are without a homeland but free to wander where they will.

During an early encounter with a female member of the White People in Aquaville, Parry is told by a hotel worker that, 'They have their places' (*DK*, 127). Parry later thinks this initially dismissive phrase may subtly signal the existence of a space between the quarters, outside the control of those who maintain the divided kingdom. He speculates that the itinerant freedom of the wandering White People is a key factor in the animosity they sometimes face, and as a social group they are either invisible (generally ignored and free to cross borders) or excessively visible as scapegoats and victims of violence. Although the White People, through being 'bureaucratically dead' (*DK*, 269), offer a tantalizing glimpse of a life outside the system of segregation, Parry's involvement with them nearly leads to his actual death when the group he is travelling with is ambushed by townsfolk in the Yellow Quarter. While recovering, it becomes clear to Parry that his time with the White People did not offer a solution to the challenges he faces in trying to belong and relate to others, and that their mute and precarious existence on the margins of life is something of a dead-end. Instead, his experiences with them form part of his experiment in 'the business of living' in the divided kingdom.

Between genres: Philip K. Dick meets Voltaire

The reader's experience of immersion in a foreign element, in a new but oddly recognizable world of sensation and experiment, emerges in part from the generic experimentation and blurring that frames the action of the narrative. While providing an essentially realist narrative set in a fairly recognizable contemporary setting (neither spaceships nor supernatural beings appear), *Divided Kingdom*, through its mixture of familiarity and foreign-ness, manages to be a disquieting read, simultaneously partaking of different genres. In an online discussion for the *Guardian* newspaper before *Divided Kingdom* was published,

Thomson gave a hint about his new book: 'I tend not to say too much about what I'm working on. I did think of a way of describing it the other day, though: Philip K. Dick meets Voltaire' (Thomson, 2000). Exploring what might have been meant by this surprising conjunction of Enlightenment satire and 1960s science fiction may shed light on how Thomson's book brings together quite different artistic modes.

Since Philip K. Dick's oeuvre is distinguished by the hyper-fertility of its creative imagination, there are a host of potential parallels to Thomson's book. One Dick text, however, that seems to share a particularly strong set of correspondences with *Divided Kingdom* is the 1964 novel *Clans of the Alphane Moon*. Dick's narrative is set on a moon that has been colonized by humans who live in communities segregated according to psychiatric conditions. Among the different clans on the moon are the Paranoids or Pares who live in a militarized community in Adolfville, while people who suffer from mania or Mans have their home in Da Vinci Heights, and the Hebes who live in Gandhitown and have disorganized schizophrenia and, like Thomson's White People, are generally regarded as harmless and even revered by some for their unworldly spirituality. The different clans tend to populate different professions and civic functions, and the Paranoids are the most dangerous grouping. As Carl Freedman (1984) has convincingly argued, paranoia is a mindset Dick returns to again and again in his fiction, albeit presented as an ultimately inadequate ideological response to the powerful complex of forces and conditions that foster it, including opaque political machinations and the effects of narcotics.

If we are struck by how *Clans of the Alphane Moon* exhibits similarities to *Divided Kingdom* in terms of the dynamics of populations segregated according to their mental/behavioural disposition, then the latter's avoidance of the generic features of science fiction becomes marked. Instead of the space colonies of the future, Thomson offers a deliberate archaism in his use of a system of humours long bereft of popular credence. In an interview Thomson has spoken of this turn to the past:

I liked the fact that a government involved in a piece of radical social engineering might look to the past for its inspiration. There was something so believable, or even human, about that – we always seem to think that things are worse now than they used to be – but it was also perverse. The idea that a government could reject progress so utterly seemed to contain within it the seeds of something unpredictable and quite possibly malignant. (Lawless, 2005)

Thomson's reflections here are notable for bringing together both conservative political tendencies and widely expressed feelings about the passing of time. As the quote suggests, Thomson acknowledges the common human experience of feeling that things were better in the past, and of course in the context of the novel he has provided a protagonist whose desire to return to the past is all too understandable, given the depth of his personal loss. In spite of this however, Thomson carefully balances this longing with the turn to the past embodied by the broader political 'geohumoralism' (to adopt Floyd-Wilson's term) of the Rearrangement. Despite the attractions of recreating that which has passed, and the prevalence of nostalgia in human experience, when raised to a political principle an attempted return to the archaic past can become, in Thomson's words, 'perverse' and 'quite possibly malignant', indicating that Parry's quest is really to secure a future, not to reclaim the past.

Thomson's allusion to Voltaire above may be read as a reference to the 1759 novel *Candide*, and Parry's journey across the divided kingdom shares aspects with Voltaire's eponymous hero's voyages in Europe and the Americas, testing the extent to which people live in the best of all possible worlds, as asserted by Candide's mentor Pangloss. The convergence of Philip K. Dick and Voltaire in *Divided Kingdom* signals the joining of a picaresque journey (perhaps putting a philosophical theory to the test) to the scenario of a segregated world, not a psychiatric division as seen in *Clans of the Alphane Moon*, but a deliberately archaic one based on medieval humours. As *Divided Kingdom*'s colour-coded map indicates, these events happen not on a faraway planet, but in a recognizable UK. A detailed approach to the maps perhaps risks placing too much weight on something that Thomson himself has admitted feeling ambivalent about including in the book, remarking in interview that, 'On the one hand, I thought the book could stand on its own without them, and that to include them might suggest some kind of weakness of vision. On the other hand, I know readers love maps' (Lawless, 2005). These comments suggest that the inclusion of the map is likely to be welcomed by readers but that the map itself is not fundamental to the book's success as a literary novel, and may risk becoming a distraction from the book's central exploration of Parry. The popularity of maps in fantasy fiction, and *Divided Kingdom*'s lack of interest in key features of fantasy writing (such as magic), may also be a factor in Thomson's ambivalence. Nevertheless, *Divided Kingdom*'s map does indicate to the reader something of the book's focus. The territory of the Republic of Ireland, a potential reminder that the kingdom has already been divided, is not presented on the map and in fact, although the map follows the contours of the UK, it is noticeable that of its constituent nations only England looks to be profoundly divided. Scotland (with the exception of Dumfries and Galloway, and Thomson's town of Burnham standing in for Glasgow), Wales and Northern Ireland are each roughly speaking only in a single quarter: Phlegmatic for Wales, Choleric for Northern Ireland and Melancholic for Scotland (Burnham is located in the Choleric Yellow Quarter). England, on the other hand, is divided almost equally between the four humours, suggesting that Englishness rather than Britishness is at stake in Parry's journey, in part centred on a London divided into four zones. So while the borders between the zones do tend to follow the UK's historical 'internal' borders, it is the diversity of Englishness that is the novel's central focus.

Thomson's allusion to Philip K. Dick and his handling of the Rearranged UK in this novel might be read as signalling the book's place within the fantastic or science fiction in terms of generic categories. In interview however, Thomson has been keen to reject the idea of a parallel world: 'None of my books are set in parallel worlds – though critics frequently describe them as exactly that. The worlds in which I set my fiction are all around you, if only you look carefully enough.' (Lawless, 2005). Thomson, one might say, is interested in more frequent and resonant intersections between his fictional world and the real one than a 'parallel' world would permit. In terms of genre, like many of Thomson's books, *Divided Kingdom* challenges and blurs strict distinctions between realism and fantasy, and operates at the intersection of philosophical writers like Voltaire, modernist innovators like Jean Rhys, and pulp sci-fi writers like Philip K. Dick. The author has claimed in interview that 'I want to be able to look at reality from a standpoint that feels unpredictable, surreal, and yet, at the same time, entirely cogent. I seem to be attracted to ideas that allow me to do this' (Hynes, 2006), and the complex system of the divided kingdom is clearly designed to produce such opportunities. Thomson's fictional experimentation traverses generic boundaries and interrogates the very nature of borders as both constitutive of identity and dangerously limiting, maintaining for the reader a balance between disorientation and strangeness on the one hand and familiarity and security on the other.

The architecture of division

If Cold War paranoia found one vibrant outlet in the science fiction of Philip K. Dick, one reference point for Thomson when he was writing *Divided Kingdom*, then what is perhaps the most powerful icon of the Cold War would seem another important influence on the form of Thomson's novel. The building of the Berlin Wall in 1961 following the city's division into four foreign-controlled zones in 1945, mirroring the division of Germany into four occupation zones by the victorious Allies after the Second World War, forms a key historical precedent for Thomson's Rearrangement, and the barricades and checkpoints Parry sees are strongly reminiscent of Berlin's systems of separation. Dutch architect Rem Koolhaas's monumental book *S, M, L, XL* (with Bruce Mau, 1998) is listed in *Divided Kingdom*'s acknowledgements and Koolhaas's reflections in the book on a 1971 visit to the Berlin Wall, which he unexpectedly describes as '*heartbreakingly beautiful*' (Koolhaas and Mau, 1998: 222), may provide some insight into the emotional impact political and architectural division has in Thomson's narrative. For Koolhaas the Berlin Wall reveals an uncomfortable duality fundamental to architecture as a practice:

The Berlin Wall was a very graphic demonstration of the power of architecture and some if its unpleasant consequences.
    Were not division, enclosure (i.e. imprisonment), and exclusion –
which defined the wall's performance and explained its efficiency –
the essential stratagems of *any* architecture?... *The wall suggested that
architecture's beauty was directly proportional to its horror.* (Koolhaas
and Mau, 1998: 226)

The duality Koolhaas apprehends in the power of the Berlin Wall, I
would contend, corresponds to the duality Thomson creates in his
exploration of borders and security in *Divided Kingdom*, where structures that apparently exist to protect end up imprisoning. The para-
doxical 'success' of a border in isolating the subject can produce both
beneficial and harmful effects.

One important difference between Thomson's *Divided Kingdom*
and post-war Germany and Berlin is that Thomson's kingdom was not
carved up by invading forces but deliberately divided by internal powers. The apparent willingness of the people to engage in this division
points to another of Koolhaas's projects launched the year after he visited Berlin, entitled 'Exodus, or the Voluntary Prisoners of Architecture'. 'Exodus', composed of a mixture of text and photomontage, was
shown at the Architectural Association in London and offered a speculative reorganization of that city. Its Prologue tells a very Berlin-like
story of a city divided in half, with a large wall built to stop people in
the Bad Half getting into the Good Half. 'Exodus' proposes to reverse
the polarity of this exercise of architectural power: 'Division, isolation, inequality, aggression, destruction, all the negative aspects of the
Wall, could be the ingredients of a new phenomenon' (Koolhaas and
Mau, 1998: 5). A speculative new reorganization of London through
the imposition of a linear Strip over the city will produce 'voluntary
prisoners' who will enjoy their seclusion within the confines of the
structure and its architectural marvels. The fantasy aspect of some
of Koolhaas's creations in 'Exodus' makes for potentially striking an-
ticipations of Thomson's kingdom, including the Park of the Four Elements, whose features evoke some of the iconic institutions visited
by Parry in each quarter. The Water sector of the Park of the Four
Elements (Koolhaas and Mau, 1998: 12) involves a large pool with a

wave machine similar to The Underground Ocean that Parry sees in Aquaville (Koolhaas and Mau, 1998: 105) and the private booths of 'Exodus's Baths, designed to bring 'hidden motivations, desires and impulses to the surface to be refined for recognition, provocation and development' (Koolhaas and Mau, 1998: 13) may be a precursor to *Divided Kingdom's* Bathysphere. Indeed Thomson's reproduction of signage in block capitals for THE UNDERGROUND OCEAN (*DK*, 105), and with extra spacing for T H E B A T H Y S P H E R E (*DK*, 114) echoes Koolhaas's presentation of the different spaces of 'Exodus', while also sustaining Parry's status as both a literal interpreter of signs, and someone who in a more generalized way struggles to decipher the world around him.

In one of many acts of uncertain decoding in the novel, Parry is initially puzzled by the flyer for the Bathysphere he is handed by a stranger at Aquaville's train station on an official visit to the Blue Quarter:

> It could be a new restaurant, I thought, or a bar. Or it might be a show. I studied the card more closely – the name and address written in dimly visible steel-grey, the background midnight-blue – then lifted my eyes to the window again. I remembered bathyspheres from adventure stories I had read when I was young. Round metal contraptions, large enough to hold a person, they were designed to be lowered to the bottom of the sea. (*DK*, 104)

This lack of certainty as to the Bathysphere's function persists during his visit to the address on the card, which seems quiet for a club. The word's link to childhood memories might be read as a factor in Parry's decision to visit the place, given his experience of separation from his parents. Parry enters while not fully understanding its purpose, and when faced with three doors to choose from, ends up selecting the one that seems to be the most popular, judging by the marks on the carpet. One might speculate that the doors denote the past, the present and the future, with a voyage into the past as the most popular choice, and Parry's experience in the booth, perhaps under the influence of a drug administered through a needle on the door handle, shows him a vision of his schoolfriend Jones before he sees a young

woman resembling his adoptive sister Marie at a young age. The se-
renity he feels in the woman's company is a powerful testament to
Parry's longing for the past:

> It didn't matter where we were going. Our destination didn't interest
> me at all. I just wanted everything to remain exactly as it was.
> I wanted it to last for ever. (*DK*, 119)

The attraction but impossibility of stasis is made clear to Parry when
he abruptly wakes up feeling nauseous several hours later alone on the
street. He returns to the Bathysphere again, having been warned by a
colleague that 'it can be a bit addictive' (*DK*, 123), this time experi-
encing his old house and hearing his mother calling him from downstairs. In the aftermath of his vision, Parry believes that 'something
quite miraculous' has occurred and that he has been changed by his
experience:

> I had gained access to a part of me that I had assumed was gone for
> ever. The club's name conveyed exactly what was being offered: a
> journey into the depths, a probing of the latent, the forbidden, the
> impenetrable. (*DK*, 136)

This psychic journey in the Bathysphere has put Parry in touch with
repressed feelings and memories, encouraging him to embrace the
unexpected and join his colleagues on a surprise trip to the Yellow
Quarter to celebrate Rearrangement Day. The trip marks Parry's decision to start taking opportunities to elude the constraints of official-
dom, and to continue his voyage in the dark.

While Parry's journey across the Divided Kingdom takes in some
special places that embody qualities specific to that quarter, including the Underground Ocean in the Blue Quarter and the Museum of
Tears in the Green Quarter, many of his experiences are fairly mundane, or at least they would be if Parry did not have to concentrate on
fitting into his new environment. The novel almost invariably positions Parry as the stranger in a strange land, forever in exile from a
country that no longer exists, an analogue for the reader's own sense
of disorientation in the rearranged kingdom. The travel aspect of the
narrative recalls eighteenth-century fiction and Mikhail Bakhtin's dis-

cussion of the differing chronotopes of writing in *The Dialogic Imagination* provides a productive framework within which to consider *Divided Kingdom*'s unconventional use of time and space:

> The device of 'not understanding' – deliberate on the part of the author, simpleminded and naive on the part of the protagonist – always takes on great organizing potential when an exposure of vulgar conventionality is involved. Conventions thus exposed – in everyday life, mores, politics, art and so on – are usually portrayed from the point of view of a man who neither participates in nor understands them. The device of 'not understanding' was widely employed in the eighteenth century to expose 'feudal unreasonableness' (there are well-known examples in Voltaire... Swift in his *Gulliver's Travels*, makes use of this device in a great variety of ways). (Bakhtin, 1981: 164)

Unlike his literary predecessors Thomson's use of 'not understanding' does not neatly fit the category of feudal unreasonableness, and his method marks a development beyond Bakhtin's typology in at least two respects.

The first is the issue of simpleminded naivety on the part of the protagonist: Parry's development is shaped by his traumatic separation from his birth family and much of his subsequent life has echoes of a child trying to adapt to new circumstances. As Thomson has described in interview:

> One of the central dynamics of the book is Thomas's various attempts to work out the difference between what he used to be and what he has become. The trouble is, the previous version of himself only lasted eight or nine years, and never developed into anything concrete or mature. What he is trying to discover is something that is unformed – a potential. At times, he almost loses himself in the gap between the two. (Lawless, 2005)

The consequence of this is that *Divided Kingdom* focuses on Parry's growing self-knowledge and understanding of the world rather than persistent ignorance, a learning process that while dangerous may also be necessary if he is to develop as a person. His sensations in the Bathysphere, while presenting visions of the past, have also changed his attitude to the present, where he experiences 'an abrupt and pronounced sense of opportunity' (*DK*, 140). It is by 'exploiting the situation to my advantage' (*DK*, 140) that Parry will make his way in the world. The second divergence from the pattern seen by Bakhtin in Voltaire and Swift is the question of participation. As I have already explored, Thomson's protagonist immerses himself in the foreign element, and is a participant (however ill-informed) rather than a voyeuristic tourist. Once Parry leaves behind the diplomatic mission to Aquaville, the laws of separation mean that he is not permitted to be the foreign observer (although he later learns that his government has been tracking him at least some of the time) and must instead simulate the 'natives', to think and behave like them and so avoid detection. His picaresque journey leaves him at the mercy of the strangers he encounters and he is both the victim of exploitation and the recipient of charity. Franco Moretti's account of borders in *Atlas of the European Novel: 1800–1900* (1998) provides a helpful analysis of two kinds of border-crossing:

> Borders, then. Of which there are two kinds: external ones, between state and state; and internal ones, within a given state. In the first case, the border is the site of *adventure*: one crosses the line, and is face to face with the unknown, often the enemy; the story enters a space of danger, surprises, suspense…
>
> *Internal* borders work differently, and focus on a theme that is far less flamboyant than adventure, but more disturbing: *treason*. (Moretti, 1998: 35–7)

It is part of the ambiguity of Thomson's novel that the borders of the divided kingdom are to a degree both external and internal: the system of segregation is upheld by all four quarters and Parry encounters the ritual burning of emblems of the four zones in a rural part of the Yellow Quarter, a community engaged in 'a kind of treason' (*DK*, 166) against the Rearrangement. As one might expect of a novel so attentive to the reversibility of value in the case of borders and security, this spectacle of treason he enjoys witnessing soon returns to bite Parry as he himself is betrayed by people he meets at the event who offer him a lift and then violently rob him. His assailants cannot resist pointing out the inadequacy of his ability to read situations and the extent of his ignorance, telling him 'if you knew it all you wouldn't have got yourself into this situation in the first place' (*DK*, 173).

Divided Kingdom as a spatial story

Divided Kingdom's combination of picaresque adventure and speculative geography is often tied up with the law, and the projection of sovereignty over territory. The work of Gilles Deleuze on nomads and the space of the state, and the distinction between smooth and striated space in Deleuze and Guattari's *A Thousand Plateaus* (1987) are potentially apposite here, however Michel de Certeau's influential book *The Practice of Everyday Life* (1984) may offer a more direct means of theorizing Parry's journey through the quarters. In a chapter entitled 'Spatial Stories' de Certeau contrasts his notion of place (*lieu*) with that of space (*espace*) (de Certeau, 1984: 117). For de Certeau, place is an indication of stability, where 'the law of the proper' operates and things are in their correct place. Space on the other hand is practiced place, based on the intersection of mobile elements, and is defined by how people make use of a location. This distinction is elaborated in his discussion of maps and tours as divergent methods of speaking or writing about place/space, with maps offering an abstract tableau that erases the itineraries that generated the raw information. Against the law of the proper, where everything is in its place (and not elsewhere), de Certeau proposes an exploration of 'delinquent' narratives:

> If the delinquent exists only by displacing itself, if its specific mark is to live not on the margins but in the interstices of the codes that it undoes and displaces, if it is characterized by the privilege of the *tour* over the *state*, then the story is delinquent. Social delinquency consists in taking the story literally, in making it the principle of physical existence where a society no longer offers to subjects or groups symbolic outlets and expectations of spaces, where there is no longer any alternative to disciplinary falling-into-line or illegal drifting away, that is, one form or another of prison and wandering outside the pale. (de Certeau, 1984: 130)

In *Divided Kingdom*, Parry's 'tour' is precisely what is placed in opposition to the state's system of separation and division, and his 'delinquent' journey, shaped by unpredictable help and hindrance from the people he meets is the means by which Parry may try to evade the falling-into-line that characterizes social conformity in the quarters. Developing de Certeau's account further in relation to the text, we can say that Parry's journey is a manifestation and expression of his social delinquency, and a product of his desire to avoid both the 'prison' of life in the Red Quarter and the illegal drifting away of the White People, who are left to wander on the edges of society. Parry attempts to live, in de Certeau's phrase, 'in the interstices of the codes' that structure the divided kingdom through mastering the differences each separate zone is designed to express.

In terms of emotional charge, the wandering 'tour' that Parry and the reader follow maintains a careful balance between threat and intrigue, between the anxiety produced by the unfamiliar and the dangerous on the one hand, and the seduction and liberation of the new on the other. To be a stranger is to be vulnerable, and as Parry is warned by the attendant at the Bathysphere in Aquaville, 'You're choosing without knowing what you're choosing. You're taking a chance. You're going into the unknown' (*DK*, 116). Looked at from this perspective, Thomson's narrator is the reader's guide on an unpredictable journey, so that the novel performs an insistent probing of the importance of security, and its dual role as a nurturing, protective force and as a rigid, imprisoning structure (the dual role of secrecy is explored in similar ways in *Secrecy*). Security, in the form of some boundaries and limits is a fundamental requirement, however the opportunity to exceed limits, cross borders and encounter novelty and alterity is also required. The abduction described in *The Book of Revelation* is, among other things, an exercise in oppressive nurturing, an evil cradling, to borrow from the title of Beirut hostage Brian Keenan's (1993) memoir. 'Border games' in *Divided Kingdom*, where Parry must play a new role each time he wishes to cross a border, are the opposite of the aggressive tribal football encounters that accompany what a newspaper vendor calls an 'important game' (*DK*, 346). Instead, Parry's multiple border games are steps, against a background of security, on the road to possibility and a different future. Viewed in this light, *Divided Kingdom* anticipates the unpredictable international wanderings of the eponymous heroine of Thomson's most recent novel *Katherine Carlyle* (2015), in which a young woman embarks on an 'experiment with coincidence' and leaves the security of her family life behind.

The sense of an ending

It is perhaps in his novels' endings that the unconventionality of Thomson's work is at its clearest, and *Divided Kingdom* is no exception. In its rejection of customary or predictable resolutions that are themselves apparently opposed, we can see how Thomson's fiction pursues its own path at the interstices of established literary conventions. The quest for his missing mother and for the re-establishment of lost family bonds that Thomas initially embarks upon becomes less important as the narrative progresses, and the novel does not conclude by staging the longed-for reunion with the mother and offering a return to some kind of prelapsarian state. Such an ending would have fallen within the conventions of what Bakhtin calls the family novel:

> The [family] novel's movement takes the main hero (or heroes) out of the great but alien world of random occurrence into the small but secure and stable little world of the family, where nothing is foreign, or accidental or incomprehensible, where authentically human relationships are re-established, where the ancient matrices are re-established on a family base: love, marriage, childbearing, a peaceful old age for the in-laws, shared meals around the family table. (Bakhtin, 1981: 232)

Unlike many literary classics of the nineteenth century, such as *Jane Eyre* or *David Copperfield*, *Divided Kingdom* leaves the family matrix permanently incomplete. Thomson's novel offers neither a family resolution nor a 'solution' to the political divisions of the country: Parry will not become a revolutionary hero to overthrow the Rearrangement and generate a (national) reunion and a return to a prelapsarian (nation) state. Bakhtin's discussion of the theory that the nineteenth-century novel existed to educate the reader for life in bourgeois capitalist society offers a useful description of such scenarios:

> This educative process is connected with a severing of all previous ties with the idyllic, that is, it has to do with man's *expatriation*. Here the process of a man's re-education is interwoven with the process of society's breakdown and reconstruction. (Bakhtin, 1981: 234)

Expatriation is an excellent term for what goes on in *Divided Kingdom*, and indeed elsewhere in Thomson's oeuvre. However, despite Parry's 're-education' in the wide world there is little sign of the kingdom's breakdown and reconstruction along new lines. As Moretti has argued:

> Internal borders define modern states as composite structures, then, made of many temporal layers; as *historical* states – that need historical novels.
> But need them to do what? To present internal unevenness, no doubt, and then, to *abolish* it. Historical novels are not just stories 'of' the border, but of its erasure, and of the incorporation of the internal periphery in the larger unit of the state: a process that mixes consent and coercion. (Moretti, 1998: 40)

Divided Kingdom by contrast is conspicuous by the persistence of unevenness and internal borders, and by the lack of an emergent subsuming national context. Parry's expulsion from the idyll does not lead to national salvation and the constitution of a new order of things, but to the prospect of a fulfilling romantic relationship and unobtrusive and private subversion: 'We would be undermining the system, of course – its ethos, its integrity… We'd be making a mockery of it. I don't care, though, not any more. I owe the system nothing' (*DK*, 395).

On the other hand, while Thomson begins his novel with the epigraph from Rhys, by the end of it he has granted his protagonist a fate far happier than that suffered by most of Rhys's expatriate heroines. The anticipated destructive suicide of Antoinette in *Wide Sargasso Sea*, Sasha's descent into alcoholism and penury in Paris in

Good Morning Midnight and the death of Anna Morgan after an illegal abortion in the original ending of *Voyage in the Dark* collectively attest to the suffering and extermination of those who exist between worlds, whose connections to place are attenuated and multiple, and who are 'misfits' according to narrow notions of what is proper. The tragic undoing of these heroines is part of Rhys's humane and searing indictment of mores, and 'she is most scathing about what she sees as the English bourgeois desire for conformity' (Carr, 2003: 104). Between the conventional kinds of victory and defeat that Thomson eschews, there is instead in *Divided Kingdom* an attempt to normalize relations between the different sides of Parry's self, and to create the possibility of mobility, experimentation and growth. By the end of the novel Thomson's hero has gained a new insight into the arrangement of the zones as 'an order of things', a particular regime, rather than the truth of existence or a destiny. He learns how to exist productively at the interstices of the zones, and realizes his potential to move and change, not to fall-in-line or become lost in the White People's 'pocket of history'. The novel ends with him imagining telling his birth parents '*I'm going to be alright*' as he is taken away from them (*DK*, 396).

In Thomson's surprising narrative, to exist between places is not to be doomed to destruction, as so often occurs in the works of Jean Rhys, who once described herself as a doormat in a world of boots, but nor is it necessarily a predicament requiring the re-establishment of lost family ties or revolutionary reform. In *Divided Kingdom* – this book that moves between dream and reality, between Rhys, Dick and Voltaire – to exist between zones is to learn how to use space rather than being fixed in place, to experiment with change and mobility and so ultimately to learn how to practice everyday life.

Note

1 'Is it true,' she said, 'that England is like a dream? Because one of my friends who married an Englishman wrote and told me so. She said this place London is like a cold dark dream sometimes. I want to wake up.'
  'Well,' I answered annoyed, 'that is precisely how your beautiful island seems to me, quite unreal and like a dream.' (Rhys, 1997: 49)

Works Cited

Bakhtin, Mikhail (1981) *The Dialogic Imagination*, ed. Michael Holquist, trans. Caryl Emerson and Michael Holquist. Austin: University of Texas Press.

Carr, Helen (2003) 'Jean Rhys: West Indian Intellectual', in Bill Schwarz (ed.) *West Indian Intellectuals in Britain*. Manchester: Manchester University Press.

de Certeau, Michel (1984) *The Practice of Everyday Life*, trans. Steven Rendall. Berkeley: University of California Press.

Deleuze, Gilles and Felix Guattari (1987) *A Thousand Plateaus: Capitalism and Schizophrenia*, trans. Brian Massumi. Minneapolis: University of Minnesota Press.

Dick, Philip K. (1964) *Clans of the Alphane Moon*. New York: Ace Books.

Floyd-Wilson, Mary (2003) *English Ethnicity and Race in Early Modern Drama*. Cambridge: Cambridge University Press.

Freedman, Carl (1984) 'Towards a Theory of Paranoia: The Science Fiction of Philip K. Dick', *Science Fiction Studies* 11(1): 15–24.

Hynes, James (2006) 'The Dreamlife of Rupert Thomson', *Boston Review*, 1 March, URL (consulted November 2014): http://www.bostonreview.net/hynes-the-dreamlife-of-rupert-thomson

Keenan, Brian (1993) *An Evil Cradling*. London: Vintage.

Koolhaas, Rem and Bruce Mau (1998) *S, M, L, XL*. New York: Monacelli Press.

Lawless, Andrew (2005) 'On the Brink of Believability: Rupert Thomson's *Divided Kingdom*', *Three Monkeys Online Magazine*, URL (consulted November 2014): http://www.threemonkeysonline.com/on-the-brink-of-believability-rupert-thomsons-divided-kingdom/

Moretti, Franco (1998) *Atlas of the European Novel: 1800–1900*. London: Verso.

Rhys, Jean (1969) *Voyage in the Dark*. Harmondsworth: Penguin (first published 1934).

Rhys, Jean (1997) *Wide Sargasso Sea*. Harmondsworth: Penguin (first published 1966).

Rhys, Jean (2000) *Good Morning Midnight*. Harmondsworth: Penguin (first published 1939).

Thomson, Rupert (2000) *Guardian* online discussion, 10 July, URL (consulted November 2014): http://www.theguardian.com/books/2000/jul/10/fiction

Voltaire (2007) *Candide*, trans. Norman Cameron. London: Penguin.

'PERHAPS THAT IS WHAT IS MEANT BY THE WORD "HAUNTED"'
POWER, DYSTOPIA AND THE GHOSTLY OTHER IN *DIVIDED KINGDOM*

Iain Robinson

In the fourth part of Rupert Thomson's novel *Divided Kingdom*, the narrator, Thomas Parry, having been attacked and robbed while on the run, takes refuge in an abandoned asylum. It strikes Parry, who has embarked on a picaresque and illicit journey around the kingdom's four quarters, as 'odd that the asylum hadn't been put to better use' (*DK*, 179), and it is not long after this reflection that he stumbles upon a rural portion of one of the borders that divide up the kingdom, 'a single concrete wall reaching away in both directions' (*DK*, 179). The reader at this point might theorize that the reason the asylum is empty is because the governing logic of the radical social plan known as The Rearrangement dictates that it is no longer needed, the divided kingdom has become the asylum, with the whole population of a future Britain having been classified 'into four distinct groups [...], according to psychology, according to type' (*DK*, 9). These groups are the four humours – the medieval medicinal temperaments – so that the population is divided into choleric, melancholic, phlegmatic and sanguine personalities, each one represented by an animal symbol and a colour, and each with its own quarter and slice of the capital city. This results in a dystopia of sorts, a bad (*dys*) place (*topos*), a genre which has generally been used as a means of providing a social critique, a warning as to how bad society might become.[1] Dystopian themes are brought to the fore, with the citizens of each sector having to partake in a kind of Orwellian doublethink in order to repress their former selves, and with movements between the four sectors of the kingdom tightly controlled. This chapter will examine the way the power structures of this fictional society are incomplete, the inscription of the individual not total, allowing for utopian potentialities, or what Michel Foucault (1998: 96) in *The Will to Knowledge* describes as 'mobile and transitory points of resistance.'[2] It will also examine the function of haunting in the novel and how Thomas Parry's journey through spectrality, and his encounters with ghostly otherness, results in a triumph of faith over cynicism in the face of the unverifiable nature of spectral presence. As Andrew Smith (2007: 147) suggests, 'the spectre is an absent presence', that which is seen but not touched, is felt but not seen, is seen to speak but cannot be heard: inherent contradictions which find their metaphor in memory, and in particular traumatic memory, which like the spectre, is marked by repetition. This chapter will argue that such haunting, traumatic memory, cannot be fully contained or repressed by the power-relations of the divided kingdom, and that Thomas Parry's quest to commune with spectrality, with his lost self, amounts to an attempt to rearticulate that which has become disjointed by the dystopian society.

Power, pantopticism, and the rearrangement

In *Discipline and Punish* (1991) Michel Foucault describes the shift from a feudal, princely model of power, based on torture, execution, and bodily incarceration, towards a model of institutional disciplinary power, which finds its symbol in the Panopticon, embodying a shift from power over the body to power over the mind. Foucault's famous evocation of a plague-stricken town subjected to a discipline-blockade describes an 'enclosed, segmented space, observed at every point, in which the individuals are inserted in a fixed place, in which the slightest movements are supervised, in which all events are recorded' (Foucault, 1991a: 197). In Thomson's novel the spatial partitioning has been achieved and maintained through force, the concrete border walls 'reinforced with watch-towers, axial crosses and even, in some areas, with mine-fields' (*DK*, 28). Foucault (1991a: 205) describes the discipline-blockade as a response to 'an exceptional situation: against an extraordinary evil'. In the minds of those in charge of The Rearrangement of the divided kingdom it is a time for 'extreme measures' (*DK*, 8) against a pathological plague that had resulted in 'a place defined by envy, misery and greed' (*DK*, 8). It is a place of routine psychological screening, where an Internal Security Act allows lengthy arrest without trial, and where, it is rumoured, trips to secret detention centres can end up being a one-way journey to an unmarked grave. The lengths that the authorities of the four quarters have gone to in order to partition their populaces are, officially at least, to prevent 'psychological contamination' (*DK*, 28), applying the discourse of contagion to psychology. It is tempting to view this exercise of power in the light of the plague-stricken town; as in Foucault's (1991a: 205) model, 'it separates, it immobilizes, it partitions'. However, despite the all too visible architecture of power and partition in *Divided Kingdom*, and the closed nature of its segments, the disciplinary power does not depend wholly upon the discipline-blockade, but is rather more *panoptic* in nature than it might at first appear.

The border watch-tower and the concrete wall are emblematic of this panoptic power mechanism. From his bedroom window, in a de-familiarized London seemingly haunted by the psychogeographical overlay of cold-war Berlin, Parry is unable to 'see any checkpoints or watch-towers', but he knows they are 'lodged deep in the jumble of buildings' and that to imagine otherwise would be 'an illusion' (*DK*, 384). The watch-tower, like the central tower of Bentham's panopticon, or the invisible but ever present Breach in China Miéville's *The City & the City*, is the symbolic locus of a disciplinary power-relation from which the citizens of the four quarters know that they will be observed, classified and punished, resulting in a self-governing behaviour that conforms to 'type'. Like the panoptic schema described by Foucault (1991a: 201) the power is 'visible and unverifiable' so that the citizen is unable to confirm that they are being observed and yet is always aware, and fearful, of the consequences of its possibility. The border walls in the divided kingdom are internalized, demarcating the pre- and post-rearrangement selves, compartmentalizing the private and the social realms of human subjectivity. The watch-tower and the border wall do not need to be seen in order for their disciplinary effect to be felt. Parry, when visiting a conference in the Blue Quarter, prepares a paper containing the possibly subversive suggestion that once instituted 'the divided kingdom was self-perpetuating' with each of the four quarters developing 'its own unique character', as the populace 'take on the attributes of that environment' (*DK*, 144). In an interview discussing national identity, Foucault (2007: 180) suggested that 'the individual is not a pre-given entity which is seized on by the exercise of power' but rather 'the product of a relation of power exercised over bodies, multiplicities, movements, desires, forces'. Parry's argument is similar in its suggestion that the attributes of the humours, into which the populace has been classified, are not innate, but rather that their personalities align to these predetermined classifications. The reason for this alignment might be considered the result of a disciplinary power-relation which seems poised between the static, closed model of Foucault's discipline-blockade and the more insidious effects of Foucault's panoptic power, of 'a society penetrated through and through with disciplinary mechanisms' (Foucault, 1991a: 209). However, the novel's psycho-geographical regard for space and landscape, as well as the more mystical references to leylines and 'alternative geography' (*DK*, 281), speak of other possible interactions between space and identity, and present a landscape haunted by traumatic memory.

The effect of power-relations on individuals is a marked one. Parry's memory begins with his traumatic night-time removal from his parents by soldiers implementing The Rearrangement. Classified as sanguine, he grows up in the Red Quarter, and rises to a position of relative trust within the regime, sharing this characteristic with other dystopian protagonists such as D-503 in Yevgeny Zamyatin's *We* (1921). This trust first takes him into the phlegmatic Blue Quarter as a conference delegate, and then to a surprise visit to the choleric

Yellow Quarter. Here, Parry, already troubled by apparitions from his past and 'a feeling of incompleteness' (*DK*, 9), uses a terrorist attack on his hotel as an opportunity to disappear and embark on a picaresque quest around the divided kingdom in search of the repressed memories of his pre-Rearrangement childhood. Parry visits all four quarters, and with each border crossing his temperament shifts into type, so that he yearns for mystical revelation in the Blue Quarter, becomes capable of rash and even violent action in the Yellow Quarter, and enters a state of grief in the Green Quarter. Each border crossing constitutes a kind of death and rebirth, suggesting individual subjectivity is fluid, susceptible to the power-relations of each quarter. Despite this, Parry remains in search of that 'special substance that makes each of us unique', proposing that it is 'finite, ethereal', that it can be 'whittled away' or 'used up altogether' as a result of traumatic experience (*DK*, 350). Many of the individuals encountered by Parry in the novel are post-traumatic subjectivities, their personal lives devastated by The Rearrangement. Victor, Parry's new father, assigned to him by the state, is mourning the loss of his wife Jean, who has been sent to another quarter, and yet is at the same time supposed to be sanguine, optimistic by nature. Victor remembers 'how happy, how very happy' (*DK*, 43) he and his wife had been before The Rearrangement and makes a book from his wife's old shoes, which are all he has left of her, 'like a photograph album' (*DK*, 43). This act is every bit as dangerous and transgressive as D-503's keeping of a journal in Zamyatin's *We*, as it reveals the extent of his grief and opens up the possibility of exposure to the authorities.[3] There is something inherently contradictory in the logic of The Rearrangement in that the very mechanism designed to bring equilibrium to the nation's humours results in personalities altered by the trauma of removal and separation, and in individuals that are forced to relive their trauma through the pain of a loss which cannot be expressed openly:

> It must have been exhausting, I thought, to have had to keep himself so hidden, while at the same time being compelled to work, to live, to function normally, but then I suspected that he, like so many others, had become used to leading a double life. The Rearrangement had

created a climate of suspicion and denial – even here, in this most open and cheerful of countries. People had buried the parts of their personalities that didn't fit. Their secrets had flourished in the warm damp earth, and it was by those secrets that they could be judged and then condemned. (*DK*, 44)

Parry's description is reminiscent of the sort of self-governing be-haviour resulting from the panoptic schema for power outlined by Foucault in that 'without any physical instrument' other than the symbolism of the borders, already discussed, 'it acts directly on indi-viduals; it gives "power of mind over mind"' (Foucault, 1991a: 206). Outwardly Parry behaves in character, and yet his childhood 'border games' with his friend Bracewell reveal something more subversive, as they practice escape, evasion, and capture, which he later reflects might have been 'some kind of dress rehearsal for the real thing' (*DK*, 58). He lives in a country that had 'been dismembered, families had been torn apart' (*DK*, 23) and Parry forces the traumatic recollec-tion of the separation from his parents and the life that preceded it 'to the very darkest corner' (*DK*, 23) of his memory in order to behave in character. However, the existence of such trauma, and the strain of leading a double-life, undermines the foundations of The Rearrangment, so that the effect of disciplinary power is incomplete, the inscription of the individual partial. Dream-life and the uncon-scious mind cannot be repressed forever, and Parry's identity crisis and personal rebellion are precipitated when the dark corners of his mind begin to reappear. Even before Parry makes his first border crossing into the Blue Quarter, he dreams of his childhood friend Jones, whose fate had been uncertain after he had been removed from the boarding school that served as a reorientation centre for boys as-signed to the Red Quarter:

> And then I saw a boy with light-brown hair standing motionless be-neath a tree. He didn't seem to notice me, despite the fact that I was walking towards him. He didn't see me. Not even when I stood in front of him. He was naked, I realised. Somehow this hadn't registered until that moment. I looked all around, but couldn't find his clothes.

The tree shuddered in the wind. The trunk wasn't visible, nor were the
branches, which seemed held together by some supernatural force.
   Staring out across the water, I trembled, as if the cold wind of the
dream had jumped dimensions and was in the world with me. The
boy was Jones. (*DK*, 83)

It seems significant that Parry is unable to see the tree for the leaves.
He can see what has grown, but not the structure holding it up, neither the branches nor the trunk, where the tree lays down its roots. It
functions, certainly, as a metaphor for Parry's psychology, in which
a later self, Thomas Parry, has grown over the former self, Matthew
Micklewright. The apparition in his dream, identified by Parry as
Jones, might also represent that lost former self, by the process of
what Sigmund Freud (1991: 205) terms *condensation*, whereby 'latent
elements which have something in common' are 'combined and fused
into a single unity in the manifest dream'. The boy does not see him,
but neither does Parry see himself. The cold wind of the dream jumps
dimensions, as if some aspect of his subconscious mind is making
itself known, and it is only after this that he asks the question, 'What
had become of him? Had he survived?' (*DK*, 83). He appears to be
beginning to address his former self, that part of him which had to be
repressed after The Rearrangement. Parry thus becomes the alienated
protagonist typical of the dystopian narrative.

Points of resistance

In *The Will to Knowledge*, Foucault argues that the existence of power
relationships 'depends on a multiplicity of points of resistance'
(Foucault, 1998: 95) playing 'the role of adversary, target, support or
handle in power relations'. He suggests that there is 'no single locus of
great Refusal' but rather 'a plurality of resistances, each of them a special case' (Foucault, 1998: 96). He goes on to posit that such points
of resistance produce 'cleavages in a society that shift about, fractur-
ing unities and effecting regroupings, furrowing across individuals
themselves, cutting them up and remoulding them' (Foucault, 1998:
96). Parry's journey across the divided kingdom leads to a series of

encounters with various 'points of resistance'. In the Blue Quarter he visits The Bathysphere, a nightclub which allows him to access his repressed memories exposing 'the hollowness that lay beneath a life so seemingly well ordered' (DK, 275). In the Yellow Quarter Parry witnesses the burning of animal effigies, representing the symbols of the four quarters, what one participant calls 'our little gesture of rebellion against the way things are' (DK, 164). Fernandez, a choleric civil-servant counterpart who expresses his belief 'in that great pipe dream, that we should all be able to live in the same country' (DK, 195), helps him to become a stowaway on a cargo ship. In the Green Quarter, true to the melancholic temperament, resistance seems most apparent in the Museum of Tears, where people bring samples of their tears as evidence of their grief and loss, but also as an affirmation of their once happier existences, 'as if a kind of essence had been wrung from each of them' (DK, 273). It is here that Parry, on discovering the vials containing his parents' tears, reflects that '[e]verything I had built had been revealed for what it was – mere scaffolding. Everything would have to be remade' (DK, 275). Foucault suggests that points of resistance manifest in 'an irregular fashion', and so it is in the divided kingdom. Their presence might be taken to point towards a utopian potentiality in what is otherwise described by Parry as 'a terrible place' (DK, 276) and thus a dystopia, but we might also view them as an aspect of the power-relation, necessary but not destabilizing when taken in isolation. Each point of resistance, by assuming the role of state adversary or target, helps to constitute the power-relation, which is, as Foucault points out, always relational in character. They are, according to Foucault, plural and 'present everywhere in the power network' (Foucault, 1998: 95), and like the power-relation itself, they traverse 'social stratifications and individual unities' (Foucault, 1998: 96). Individually they are weak, transitory, and easily crushed when the state has a need to demonstrate its power. This can be seen in the military response to the burning of the animal effigies. There is thus, according to Foucault (1998: 96), 'no soul of revolt'. Yet Foucault (1998: 96) also suggests it is 'the strategic codification of these points of resistance that makes a revolution possible', that the individual points might become integrated in the same way that institutions integrate the power of the state. Such revolutionary potential is most apparent in the cumulative effect that these points of resistance have on Parry, who is almost unique in having travelled across borders, and in his decision to try to step out of the power-relation by becoming one of the 'bureaucratically dead' (*DK*, 269) White People, society's untouchables. These people have no status because they have been assessed as having no humour and thus no character, and are 'allowed to cross borders at will' (*DK*, 125). Parry recognizes this as a 'licence to go wherever they pleased' (*DK*, 270) and forms a plan to steal the clothes of a White Person. As soon as he dons his disguise he begins to unmake himself, becoming altered 'in some indefinable way' (*DK*, 289). He enters 'the fold in reality that the White People inhabited' (*DK*, 291), and begins to perceive the world differently, if not completely outside of the power-relation, then at its very limits, allowed to roam relatively free from institutionalized power, 'as if the world, while looking the same, were actually reflected, diluted, a distant cousin of itself' (*DK*, 296).

In the White People it is possible to discern a curious likeness with Breach, the shadowy thought-police that oversee the twin cities of Bezel and Ul Qoma in Miéville's *The City & The City*. The twin cities coexist in the same geographical space, their territories overlapping into what Miéville terms 'crosshatching', with stretches of the city being 'broken by alterity' (Miéville, 2009: 29). In the crosshatched stretches the cities form a kind of tense double-exposure, so that in stretches of contested territory houses belonging in one city or the other might exist next to one another, or one part of a street might be in Bezel and the other in Ul Qoma. As in *Divided Kingdom*, the citizens of each state have to partake in a kind of doublethink in which they 'unsee' (see and immediately ignore) the other city. For the citizens of both cities it is at once second nature and a source of unbearable tension, in which the mere act of walking the streets involves 'unseeing' those citizens from the other city that might be encountered. To cross illegally between cities, or even to see and acknowledge the other city, is to 'breach', a crime which is monitored by Breach, who, like the White People, exist in a fold in reality, a visionary third space, but where they are able to exist at the centre of the panopticon as a higher body of enforcers, symbolic of its power. Here lies the crucial distinction between Breach and the White People. If Breach are in the tower at the heart of the Panopticon, the invisible enforcers, then the White People exist at the periphery of the Panopticon, allowed to wander across borders, present and yet absent as citizens, and for the most part ignored, except in places where their apparent freedom meets with a resentment that spills into violence. And yet a crucial similarity remains in that both are ghost-like, present and yet absent, their visibility uncertain.

Disjointed place and the ghostly other

Jude Roberts (2013: 188) suggests the 'fear and anxiety' in Miéville's book might be 'read as a comment on the massive expansion of surveillance in Britain'. I would contend that a similar reading might be made of Thomson's novel. The disciplinary power-relation, The Internal Security Act and the references to detentions without trial might be taken as allusions to the kinds of security legislation instituted by many Western governments in the wake of the terror attacks on September 11th, 2001, and thus constitute a dystopian warning as to where such legislation might lead. 'You do not have to be strong to abuse power,' one of the characters, Cody, tells Parry. 'You can abuse it out of weakness or insecurity. Out of fear' (DK, 239). Thomson's *Divided Kingdom* evokes the twentieth-century authoritarian regimes of East Germany, Latin America, and South Africa, and is in a Derridean sense haunted by them, but it is also alert to the present cultural moment.

However, haunting in *Divided Kingdom*, as is the case in a number of Thomson's other novels,[4] is no blunt instrument in a political argument. Jacques Derrida, in *Spectres of Marx*, makes the case that literary depictions of the spectral are representative of that which haunts us culturally. Understanding the function of haunting in the novel is central to making a reading of this novel as a journey through spectrality. By placing his faith in the uncertain, in the liminal, and in encounters with the ghostly other, Parry unlocks a series of psychological border crossings towards self-discovery and agency in a way that challenges the power-relations of the divided kingdom. Derrida opens *Spectres of Marx* with a deconstruction of the phrase *I would like to learn to live finally*. He suggests that to live 'is not something one learns' (Derrida, 2006: xvii) but that it is a knowledge acquired 'from the other at the edge of life' (Derrida, 2006: xvii). This 'learning to live', what he describes as 'a heterodidactics between life and death' (Derrida, 2006: xvii), is something which he proposes can only take place in the border territories between the two:[5]

> If it – learning to live – remains to be done, it can happen only between life and death. Neither in life nor in death *alone*. What happens between two, and between all the 'two's' one likes, such as between life and death, can only maintain itself with some ghost, can only *talk with or about* some ghost. (Derrida 2006, xvii)

Such a border territory is redolent of the liminality which will be familiar to Thomson's readers.[6] In *Divided Kingdom* there are a number of incidents which are suggestive of haunting and which occur in key moments of the narrative. In the old ballroom of the large house which serves as a boarding school for the children reallocated to the Red Quarter, Parry catches 'a glimpse of a trombone in the shadows' (*DK*, 7) and feels the air rustle 'as if a girl in an evening gown had just whirled by' (*DK*, 7). Intriguingly, Thomson does not have Parry describe this as a haunting but rather has him imagine that the room, perhaps like the kingdom, 'had seen happier, livelier days, and that traces of that time remained' (*DK*, 7) suggesting a sort of sensitivity to memory as haunting. A similar incident occurs after Jones is removed from the school after weeks of standing on one leg in a corridor, as if gazing 'into a world that lay beyond this one' (*DK*, 16):

> Curiously enough, the corridor he had occupied didn't seem empty after he had gone. It was as though he had left something of himself behind, a kind of imprint on the air, as though, by standing there like that, he had changed that part of the house for ever. Perhaps that's what is meant by the word 'haunted'. In any case, I never felt comfortable in that corridor again and avoided it whenever I could. (*DK*, 17)

Derrida, when describing 'learning to live with ghosts', claims that 'this being-with specters would also be, not only but also, a politics of memory, of inheritance' (Derrida, 2006: xviii). He develops this idea when analysing the way history and philosophy are haunted, suggesting that memories, like ghosts, will not stay in their places and refuse to recognize borders, 'they pass through walls, these revenants, day and night, they trick consciousness and skip generations' (Derrida, 2006: 36).

For Derrida (2006: 20), the liminality that allows haunting, or spectrality, to be experienced is largely a temporal phenomenon, 'a dislocated time of the present, at a radically disjointed time, without certain conjunction'. This 'disjointed now' (Derrida, 2006: 1) calls into doubt 'the border between the present, the actual or present reality of the present, and everything that can be opposed to it' (Derrida, 2006: 48) such as absence, virtuality and so forth. In *Divided Kingdom* this liminality finds expression in the border territories or abandoned spaces which are the locus of profound unease. These act as spatial metaphors for Parry's journey into selfhood and memory, his attempts to learn to live with ghosts. If we are to take the divided kingdom as a dystopia of sorts, then the *dys* of the *topos*, or place, might be understood not only in the sense of the *Oxford English Dictionary* definition of 'hard, bad, unlucky' (Onions, 1991: 621) but also in the sense of the *OED* definition of 'dis', of being pulled '[i]n twain, in different directions, apart, assunder' (Onions, 1991: 557), a *dys*topia or *dis*topia which is a radically disjointed place, broken, troubled – 'the country had been dismembered' (*DK*, 23). The lexicon of haunting and of the dead which features in the novel is thus associated with the language of journeys and of borders, of reaching across the broken parts of the body, to both commune with the dead, with memory, and to bring about a kind of healing. It is notable how two of the early abandoned spaces in the novel, the railway carriage where Parry first achieves orgasm and the stretch of motorway where he and Bracewell play border games, are related to transportation, but transport in ways other than the physical, to sexual ecstasy on the one hand, and to fantasies of escape on the other. We do not find any explicit references to haunting in the descriptions of these places, although it is clear that the railway carriage, in part, functions as a metaphor for suppressed memory, described as quiet in 'the way that someone who's gagged is quiet' (*DK*, 33), but then at this stage of the story Parry has yet to cross any borders or conjure any ghosts into being.

His first trip to the Blue Quarter is a different matter, prior to which he has already started to sense 'the brutal interruption' (*DK*, 82) of the uncrossed borders of his inner self. His visit to the Bathysphere allows him to cross some of these borders; he talks to Jones and hears his mother's voice calling him (a recurring motif in Thomson's writing).[7] However, neither of these encounters with the dead proves adequate to the task of helping him learn to live. They are instead a stimulus for his quest, he must make more contact, cross further borders, as he realizes that the night of his removal from his parents was not the birth he had supposed it to be:

> The cold hands, the bright lights – my parents grieving . . . I had died that night, and I'd been dead ever since. And now I was trying to do something about that. What was this whole journey in the end but an attempt to bring myself back to life?
> 'I've been dead all this time,' I said, laughing, 'and I didn't even know it.' (*DK*, 192)

That Parry considers himself, to some degree, dead, heightens the uncertainty and liminality regarding life/death, presence/absence, as he finds himself cast, to some extent, in the role of a ghost, 'like someone who has died and can't let go, someone who wants desperately to rejoin the living' (*DK*, 277). The role becomes fully apparent in the Green Quarter, where he encounters 'three scraps of white in the darkness' of a country churchyard, and realizes that these 'bureaucratically dead' White People 'instinctively identified with dead people' (*DK*, 269). It is shortly after this that he begins to formulate his plan to join the White People. The White Person whose clothes and identity he steals is described as 'a ghostly shape' (*DK*, 283). In their ability to cross borders at will, to walk through walls, the White People closely resemble ghosts, and as Parry loses himself to the White People, 'a people for whom time had no relevance at all' (*DK*, 297), he also loses a sense of present time – one of his number removes the hands from

Parry's watch – creating a further layer of liminality as temporal borders collapse; 'time began to blur' (*DK*, 309).

Derrida (2006: 221) suggests that in order to learn to live with the ghost one must learn 'how to talk with him, with her, how to let them speak or how to give them back speech, even if it is in oneself, in the other, in the other of oneself'. Parry learns to commune with the White People through telepathy, discovering the other in himself, but in doing so, he loses his own speech. It is up to Odell – a character reminiscent of I-330 in Zamyatin's *We* or Julia in Orwell's *Nineteen Eighty-Four* – to give it back to him, to bring him back to the world of the living. She does this through stories, her own life story, in a seeming affirmation of the power of storytelling, in its 'magical or spiritual dimension', in its ability to 'cast a spell over the people listening, enabling them to accomplish feats similar to those described' (*DK*, 366). He realizes that the stories have prepared him to make one final border crossing. In a further echo of Cold-War Berlin, Odell takes him to a derelict house which backs onto the border with the Red Quarter, a place haunted by traumatic memory. 'Are you dead?' (*DK*, 368) asks a young girl in a winged fancy dress costume, a fairy or an angel. The reader might well ask the same of the girl. As Derrida (2006: 369) puts it, 'one does not know if it is living or if it is dead', one is unable to verify whether these apparitions are living or dead, present or absent. Parry then sees his former housemate, Brendon Burroughs, crouching naked in a fridge, and it is again difficult to know if this is a ghostly apparition, a vision, or reality. Undecidability regarding the status of these apparitions (for appear they do) heightens the liminality of the border and also emphasizes the heterodidactive aspect of these encounters: Parry's communing with these apparitions, with the White People, with Odell, as a way of 'learning to live finally'.

The rearticulated skeleton

What, then, is the relationship between this journey through spectrality and the power relationships already described? Memories and ghosts, the dead, have no truck with totality or with borders, like

Odell or the White People they walk through such walls. As such, they defy the reach of panoptic power, existing beyond the rational, resisting analysis and thus disciplinary classification. Or as Michel de Certeau (1984: 108) argues in *The Practice of Everyday Life*, superstitions are incompatible with totalitarianism and the haunted place 'inverts the schema of the *Panopticon*' with an unseen absence (as opposed to the unseen presence of panoptic power), a counterpoint therefore to disciplinary power.[8] The ghostly other refuses to recognize the walls of totality. Both an unseen absence and a felt presence, it is a paradox, liminal and unverifiable, and thus to acknowledge and commune with it amounts to a threat to the division of the kingdom. If we consider the dystopia in *Divided Kingdom* to be as much of a disjointed place (*dis*topia) as it is a bad place (*dys*topia), a radical disjointing that marks (or inscribes) every individual with internal fissures and borders, much like Foucault's description of a plurality of resistances that produce cleavages in society and individuals, then we can see Parry's journey through spectrality as an attempt, at an instinctive and personal level, to rearticulate the disjointed skeleton, to re-unite the kingdom within himself, to learn to live with the ghosts of traumatic memory. Parry's voice returns to him once Odell helps him to cross the border, he is no longer a White Person, and reflects that he 'could hear himself' (*DK*, 375). He also finds himself wondering whether the country is overseen by 'a committee made up of representatives of all four countries', 'a rainbow cabinet' (*DK*, 381). Such unity seems to him 'logical – even necessary' (*DK*, 381), and it is such a unity that he possesses, having lived in all four quarters, having crossed all borders, having reduced himself to the role of ghost, untouchable, and returned to the living.

Siân Adiseshiah and Rupert Hildyard in their introduction to *Twenty-First Century Fiction* (2013: 10) suggest that depictions of haunting are 'an indication of contemporary feelings of dis-settlement and powerlessness, a recognition of the limits of contemporary knowledge', and Wolfgang Funk (2013: 158) suggests that such writing – he uses the example of Hilary Mantel's *Beyond Black* – shows how 'postmodernity itself is haunted and eventually defeated by the spectres of its own significant Other: an instinctive trust in signs'.

Thomson's novel reflects the present cultural moment, where the dominant structures of power, be they late-capitalist or state authoritarian, can be challenged within or at the edges of state control, as evidenced by the 'Occupy' movement and the Arab Spring revolutions, which have used social media, itself panoptic in the way it compiles and shares individual data, in order to undermine and rally against existing power-relations.[9] The lack of such technologies in Thomson's novel is marked, but so is the presence of their symbolic equivalent, the telepathic powers of the White People and Odell's teleportation, a knowledge that can be made to network and transgress the boundaries of the existing power-relation. Thomson, by having Parry place his trust in signs, finding his salvation in the White People and a girl able to teleport with the wind, is able to hint at what Funk (2013: 158) describes as 'another economy of knowledge' where 'undecidability results not in scepticism but in faith'. As Derrida (2006: 47) puts it, 'the dividing line between ghost and actuality ought to be crossed, like utopia itself, by a realization, that is, by a revolution'.[10] Parry's encounters with resistance, whether martial, symbolic, social, personal, or the decidedly Other, add up to a kind of personal rebellion. It is only after he has thoroughly lost himself as a White Person that he is able to return to the Red Quarter, guided by Odell, and is reconciled to himself, to his lack of pre-Rearrangement memory, realizing that the 'total blankness stood for something' and that it might prove 'a source of strength and comfort' if he can 'learn to trust it' (DK, 389).

It is tempting to read Thomson's seeming preoccupation with a post-traumatic subjectivity as evidence of Philip Tew's much celebrated notion of the 'traumatological', and certainly it does match Tew's description of a novel that 'responds to concrete historical conditions *and* expresses either overtly or covertly an awareness of radical simultaneous challenges to *both* personal identity and the social order' (Tew, 2007: 190). However, this would also describe effectively key tropes identifiable in some of the great works of twentieth-century dystopian fiction, those reactions to twentieth-century modernity that Raffaeli Baccolini and Tom Moylan (2003: 1) define as 'the *classical*, or canonical, form of dystopia', such as Orwell's *Nineteen Eighty-Four* and Zamyatin's *We*. As a character, Parry owes much to Orwell's

Winston Smith, who is also a man in a position of trust on the inside of the regime, similarly haunted and puzzled by memories of a childhood trauma, and desirous to make sense of his past as well as larger society. Many commentators over the past two decades have concentrated on the critical sensibility of novels partaking in the dystopian genre, novels which carry within them some element of political debate over the future direction of their fictional societies, novels in which the dystopian protagonists frequently engage in organized martial or political resistance against their dystopian circumstances.[11] Unlike such 'critical dystopias', *Divided Kingdom* is a novel that does not carry within it an overt, or even covert, political message, and neither does it foreground a single political issue, such as gender or ecology. Resistance is diffuse, scattered, a dislocated skeleton of selfhood and society which Parry reassembles only through his trust in signs, his spectral journey, and his encounters with the ghostly other. Like the other '[t]horoughly British Dystopias' identified by Tew – Will Self's *The Book of Dave* and J. G. Ballard's *Kingdom Come* – *Divided Kingdom* is no straightforward example of the genre, its border crossings suggestive of the transgressions in genre in which it partakes. With its crosshatching of elements of dystopian fiction, the picaresque novel, and fantasy writing, the novel might be better classed under the umbrella term of speculative fiction, if it can be classified at all. Towards the end of the novel Parry suggests that '[d]ifferent situations demand different narratives, and each one had its proper moment' (*DK*, 366). This novel's apparent concerns with memory, trauma, violence, border crossings, psychogeographical overlay, and haunting, might, when taken together with other novels such as Miéville's *The City & The City* or John Burnside's *Glister*, suggest the broader emergence of a literature that reframes dystopian generic traits to reflect a distinctly twenty-first-century sensibility: novels which dare to imagine other economies of knowledge in the face of the dominant power-relations of the contemporary world.

Notes

1 Lyman Tower Sargent defines the 'dystopia or negative utopia' as 'a non-existent society described in considerable detail and normally located in

time and space that the author intended a contemporaneous reader to view as considerably worse than the society in which the reader lived' (Sargent, 1994: 9).

2 Foucault (1991b: 83) describes the body as the 'inscribed surface of events'. Discursive fields (law, the family, medicine, etc), which are the product of certain power-relations and knowledge-constitutions, write and re-write the body (behaviours, psychologies, identities) like a text, a surface on which history makes its mark. Power marks us, it is the mark made upon us like writing, an inscription on our subjectivities.

3 Similarly, Winston Smith keeps a diary in George Orwell's *Nineteen Eighty-Four* (1949), and Margaret Atwood's *The Handmaid's Tale* (1986) is presented as a series of transcribed tape recordings. Tom Moylan, in *Scraps of the Untainted Sky* (2000), suggests that such actions in dystopian novels are a way of characters finding agency in the form of a counter-narrative against the dystopian state.

4 I think primarily here of *The Five Gates of Hell* (1991) and *Death of a Murderer* (2007).

5 *Heterodidactic.* Derrida is drawing from *hetero*, meaning other or different, and *didactic*, meaning to teach or instruct. The *auto*didact is self taught. With *heretordidactics* the implication is that the learning or instruction is achieved through contact with otherness.

6 To speak of liminality is to speak of 'thresholds, gateways, passages, initiation rituals and other-realms, all expanding the limits of our socially ordered world, puncturing its skin and disrupting its structure' (Sutton 2000: 18). In *The Five Gates of Hell* (1991) Thomson presents the reader with Moon Beach, a city where people come to die, where the main industry is funerals, and where most of the burials take place at sea. As such both the town and the sea (water) serve as liminal places, as do the large towers which once served as sky-scraping mausoleums. In *Death of a Murderer* (2007) the liminality is expressed not only through the main setting, a hospital morgue and autopsy room, but also in a number of spatial settings involving water, such as a tidal estuary and an Italian lake. Both novels also contain depictions of encounters with ghostly apparitions.

7 In Rupert Thomson's memoir *This Party's Got to Stop* (2010), Thomson recounts his childhood experience of hearing his recently deceased mother calling him, as he stands beneath a yew tree in his garden, '[r]eal and clear, but disembodied, like a recording - though later I thought it was how an angel might sound, if an angel were to speak' (*PGS*, 1). It is

an incident which seems to have haunted his fiction. *The Five Gates to Hell* (1991) contains an almost identical account in which one of the protagonists, Nathan, hears his dead mother's voice call him in an overgrown part of his garden, 'but there was no second call, and he turned round, and there was nobody there, not a sound, and he felt strange then, he felt as if he'd been visited' (*FGH*, 224). The motif is more disguised in *Divided Kingdom*, but shares with these other accounts the sudden, unexpected sense of visitation, and significantly, as with the other descriptions, Parry never hears the voice of his mother again.

8 'Totalitarianism attacks what it quite correctly calls *superstitions*: supererogatory semantic overlays that insert themselves "over and above" and "in excess", and annex to a past or poetic realm a part of the land the promoters of technical rationalities and financial profitabilities had reserved for themselves' (de Certeau, 1984: 106).

9 Recent examples of this phenomenon might include the organisation of the occupation of Cairo's Tahrir Square, the 'indignados' protests against austerity in Spain, and the occupation of New York's Zuccotti Park. For a detailed study see Paulo Gerbaudo (2012).

10 Derrida here is describing Marx's realization that the containment of the 'spectre of communism' by hegemony amounted to a dividing line that needed to be crossed in order for radical change to commence, but that paradoxically '[Marx] too will have continued to believe, to try to believe in the existence of this dividing line as a real limit and conceptual distinction' (Derrida, 2006: 47).

11 Perhaps the most notable critic to write on 'critical dystopia' is Tom Moylan in *Scraps of the Untainted Sky* (2000).

Works Cited

Adiseshiah, Siân and Rupert Hildyard (2013) 'Introduction: What Happens Now', in S. Adieshiah and R. Hildyard (eds) *Twenty-First Century Fiction: What Happens Now*. London: Palgrave.

Baccolini, Raffaella and Tom Moylan (2003) 'Dystopia and Histories', in R. Baccolini, and T. Moylan (eds) *Dark Horizons: Science Fiction and the Dystopian Imagination*. New York and London: Routledge.

de Certeau, Michel (1984) *The Practice of Everyday Life*, trans. S. Rendall. Berkley: University of California Press.

Derrida, Jacques (2006) *Specters of Marx*, trans. P. Kamuf. New York and London: Routledge.

Foucault, Michel (1991a) *Discipline and Punish: The Birth of the Prison*, trans. A. Sheridan. London: Penguin.

Foucault, Michel (1991b) 'Nietzsche, Genealogy, History', in Paul Rabinow (ed.) *The Foucault Reader*, pp. 76–100. London: Penguin.

Foucault, Michel (1998) *The Will to Knowledge: The History of Sexuality: 1*, trans. R. Hurley. London: Penguin.

Foucault, Michel (2007) 'Questions on Geography', trans. C. Gordon, in J. Crampton and S. Elden (eds) *Space, Knowledge and Power: Foucault and Geography*, pp. 63–77. London: Ashgate.

Freud, Sigmund (1991) *Introductory Lectures on Psychoanalysis*, trans. A. Richards. Harmondsworth: Penguin.

Funk, Wolfgang (2013) 'Ghosts of Postmodernity: Spectral Epistemology and Haunting in Hilary Mantel's *Fludd* and *Beyond Black*', in S. Adiseshiah and R. Hildyard (eds) *Twenty-First Century Fiction: What Happens Now*. London: Palgrave.

Gerbaudo, Paolo (2012) *Tweets and the Streets: Social Media and Contemporary Activism*. London: Pluto Press.

Miéville, China (2009) *The City & The City*. London: Pan Macmillan.

Moylan, Tom (2000) *Scraps of the Untainted Sky: Science Fiction, Utopia, Dystopia*. Boulder, CO: Westview Press.

Onions, C. T. (ed.) (1991) *The Shorter Oxford English Dictionary On Historical Principles: Volume 1: Third Edition*. Oxford: Clarendon Press.

Orwell, George (2004) *Nineteen Eighty-Four*. London: Penguin.

Roberts, Jude (2013) 'Crosshatching: Boundary Crossing in the Post-Millennial British Boom', in S. Adiseshiah and R. Hildyard (eds) *Twenty-First Century Fiction: What Happens Now*. London: Palgrave.

Sargent, L. T. (1994) 'The Three Faces of Utopianism Revisited', *Utopian Studies* 5(1): 1–37.

Smith, Andrew (2007) 'Hauntings', in Catherine Spooner and Emma McEvoy (eds) *The Routledge Companion to Gothic*, pp. 147–154. Abingdon: Routledge.

Sutton, P. C. (2000) 'The Textual Mutation of Liminal Attributes', in I. Soto (ed) *A Place That is Not a Place: Essays in Liminality and Text*. Madrid: Gateway Press.

Tew, Philip (2007) *The Contemporary British Novel: Second Edition*. London: Continuum.

Zamyatin, Yevgeny (1993) *We*, trans. Clarence Brown. New York: Penguin.

HAPPIER DAYS FOR ALL OF US?
CHILDHOOD AND ABUSE IN *DEATH OF A MURDERER*

Christopher Vardy

'[T]he child' is both a fetish and a flexible construction that is, to a large extent, independent of outside standards like age. Adolescents are stuffed back in to childhood when it serves our purposes, as it often does when we are talking of molestation or crime. Victims of crime as old as eighteen or nineteen can be thought of as children, whereas perpetrators as young as six can be thought of and treated as adults. Such analogical playing with categories follows our needs. [...] The child is functional, a malleable part of discourse rather than a fixed stage; 'the child' is a product of ways of perceiving, not something that is *there*. (Kincaid, 1998: 18–19)

Is it the case that in the last ten years or so, years of turmoil, children have become a new way of evading or expressing something as yet unclear? (Eaglestone, 2013: 85).

Once again, he had the feeling there was something to be discovered, but it was like having a word on the tip of your tongue and knowing you would never remember it. There were things here that couldn't be squared away – not by him, in any case (*DM*, 29).

Introduction: patterns of abuse

Billy Tyler, the protagonist of Rupert Thomson's *Death of a Murderer* (2007), remembers his ex-lover Venetia's revelation that she was sexually abused by her father as a discovery that both contaminates and transforms him:

> What he learned would alter him for ever. Certain stories lodge like rusty hooks in the soft flesh of the mind. You cannot free yourself.
> Sitting in the mortuary with his eyes shut, Billy heard the rasp of a lighter.
> 'You'd know all about that, of course,' he said. (*DM*, 196)

This quotation exemplifies the novel's associative structure. Most of the text takes place over the course of a night shift in which Billy, a police officer, guards the body of Myra Hindley in a hospital morgue. In this eerily static and isolated setting, the literal and figurative spectres of Hindley and the Moors Murders prompt and sometimes force Billy to remember moments from his own life.[1] These interactions often draw unsettling parallels between Hindley and Brady's famous crimes and Billy's seemingly 'ordinary' childhood and experiences.[2] The violent and penetrative metaphor used in the quotation to describe the transformative effects of hearing Venetia's story also underscores the disturbing and potentially disruptive power exerted by narratives of sexually abused children. Contemporary British culture is obsessed with child abuse, and consumes more and more cultural production about it. Examples include the luridly reported recent investigations into the crimes of celebrity abusers and alleged paedophile rings at the heart of government and the intelligence services, the prolonged boom in 'misery memoirs' and trauma narratives, and the increasingly routine use of paedophilia and the figure of the missing or dead child as a 'go-to' plot device in film, fiction and television drama.[3] This dizzying proliferation of child abuse narratives does more than just expose the suffering of real children and/or represent a long overdue recognition of the testimony of abuse victims. These narratives, and the patterns that they take, are structured by underlying political and historical discourses, which operate less visibly and are under-re-searched. Analysing the cultural or ideological work child abuse narratives do, or their signification within contemporary culture, might be misinterpreted as trivializing the very real suffering of victims or somehow undermining the veracity of their testimony. However, it is vitally important to be attentive to how and why the cultural 'stories' we collectively tell about abuse are *constructed* in particular ways, because the assumptions that underpin those stories are often highly conservative in their inattention to structural and social contexts for abuse, reliant on overly simplified and deterministic models of history and subjectivity, and rooted in nostalgic fantasies about childhood and children.

Throughout *Death of a Murderer* there is a recurring pattern of abused, murdered or traumatized children that extends far beyond the victims of Hindley and Brady. As well as adults like Venetia who remain determined by their histories of abuse, the novel is punctuated by missing teenagers, dead babies, and children who inexplicably commit suicide. This chapter argues that one of the novel's most fascinating and disquieting subtexts is the implication that violent crimes like the Moors Murders are not simply aberrant events, but the rarest and most extreme examples of an underlying logic or social system in which children – and, crucially for the novel and for the specific focus of this chapter, what the figure of the child and childhood *represent* – are insecure and unsafe. Thomson's novel doesn't tell stories about child abuse in the consolingly simplistic or palatable forms that commonly circulate in contemporary culture.[4] The text offers no neat explication for its pattern of abused children and arrested development. There is no Edenic fantasy of childhood and/or the recent past, threatened by a demonized, deviant other; nor are historical periods like the 1960s or 1970s indicted in uncomplicated ways. *Death of a Murderer* interrogates these simplistic narratives about child abuse. More than that, in Thomson's novel the figure of the abused child becomes a prism through which cultural investments in childhood are themselves explored and denaturalized.

This chapter will focus primarily on the text's treatment of two of these constitutive cultural narratives. First, the novel reveals the pervasive nostalgia for childhood in the recent past to be illusory and damaging: these idyllic, pre-lapsarian narratives serve contemporary needs and do little justice to either the complexities of the past or the real experiences of children. Yet the text does not replace a hagiography of childhood with an equally neat 'horror story'. Instead, childhood is presented as a difficult and anxious but also exciting and pleasurable period that determines adult life in complex ways, and which is refigured as we remember it: a seductive origin myth always in the process of being rewritten. Second, the novel destabilizes the widespread understanding of the child as an embodiment of progress, possibility and futurity. This is figured not only through the murder and abuse that leaves children 'lost in time' but through the pattern of children in the novel who are trapped in unstable lives or face uncertain futures. In *Death of a Murderer*, the figure of the abused child becomes an anxious metaphor for the power of the past – simultaneously determining and impossible to fully grasp and articulate – and for the fear of a precarious and unknowable future.

The figure of the child: uses and abuses

Before discussing how Thomson's novel figures and interrogates these two narratives, it is vital to briefly contextualize them. Why do these discourses around abuse and childhood exist in their contemporary forms, and what does the increasing ubiquity of the figure of the abused child in contemporary cultural production signify? As James Kincaid (1998: 19) argues in the first epigraph to this chapter, 'the child is functional, a malleable part of discourse rather than a fixed stage; "the child" is a product of ways of perceiving, not something that is *there*'. For Kincaid, as for critics Erica Burman, Jacqueline Rose and Daniela Caselli, the child as a *figure* does political and ideological work. Rooted as it still is in the Romantic idealization of the child as a tabula rasa, contemporary figurations of the child become sites for intense adult investment and projection, which can efface the experiences of real children:

> [The] dominant imaginaries – the sets of cultural associations and affective relations mobilised around 'the child' – oppressively occlude

the real conditions of children's lives, with the complexity and diversity of children's lives typically reduced to and abstracted (especially from class and national identifiers) into some notional, highly symbolised and usually singular (and often young and/or female) child. (Burman, 2008: 11)

David Peace, whose contemporary historical fictions are no stranger to child-as-metaphor, illustrates the incongruity between the material/corporeal and the abstracted/idealized child in typically grisly terms. When ten-year old Clare Kemplay is abducted and murdered in *Nineteen Seventy Four* (1999), her killer sews wings hacked from a live swan onto her back to transform her into 'an angel': 'skin so pale, hair so fair and wings so white' (Peace, 1999: 110). But Clare's body cannot physically support the weight of the 'angelic' wings and they become detached, tearing the skin from her back: the intensity of her killer's fetishistic investment in childhood destroys her young body.

These damaging 'cultural associations and affective relations' (Burman, 2008: 11) are historically contingent, and discourses of childhood are not only transformed and delimited by historical change but are often a means of exploring and registering anxiety about that historical change. Sociologist Chris Jenks argues that the rapid socio-economic changes of the last forty years have transformed the meaning of 'the child'. He sketches a broad transition from 'modern' notions of childhood – embodying the promise of progress and futurity – to the figure of the 'post-modern' child, a fetishized symbol of stability and a focus for backward-looking nostalgia:

> The vortex created by the quickening of social change and the alteration of our perceptions of such change mean that, whereas children used to cling to us, in modernity, for guidance into their/our 'futures', now we, through late modernity, cling to them for 'nostalgic' groundings, because such change is both intolerable and disorienting for us. They are lover, spouse, friend, workmate and, at a different level, symbolic representations of society itself. (Jenks, 2005: 112)

While Jenks's analysis of the distinct impulses behind investments in futurity and nostalgia is persuasive (and has been generative in structuring this chapter's reading of *Death of a Murderer*), his suggestion that modernity's investments in childhood have been simply super-seded by postmodernity is unconvincing, relying as it does on neat epochal periodization. In fact, as Lee Edelman notes, the symbolic future child still 'shapes the logic within which the political itself may be thought' (Edelman, 2004: 2). For Edelman (2004: 3–5), 'think-ing of the children' is a highly conservative form of social reproduc-tion: a way for hegemonic forces to preclude radical social change or transformation through the regulatory figure of the child, for whom the supposedly 'imperilled' socio-political status quo must be shored up. Whether one agrees entirely with Edelman's claims about this moralistic 'reproductive futurism', the ongoing function of the figure of the child in structuring discourses of social and political futurity is difficult to dispute. One example is the ongoing debate about auster-ity, which is invariably framed by both sides through discussions of our collective abstracted future 'children, and their children's children' either burdened with debt or stymied by inadequate public services for generations to come. Edelman, combining psychoanalytic and Foucauldian insights, persuasively defines the contemporary figure of the 'child' as a 'disciplinary Image' of *both* an 'imaginary past' and a 'site of projective identification with an always impossible future' (Edelman, 2004: 31). The child simultaneously represents a myth of pure historical origin and a site for fantasy about collective futures.

So, if in many crucial ways the child's association with progressive futurity is still with us, what *has* changed in late twentieth- and early twenty-first-century culture? Unlike Jenks's neat periodization, the political philosopher Wendy Brown (2001: 3) offers a more nuanced model of historical change, arguing that in the contemporary world, the 'constitutive' collective meta-narratives of modernity – specifi-cally those of the sovereign subject, rights-based freedoms, and te-leological/progressive models of history and temporality – have been *destabilized* but not *replaced*: they 'remain those by which we live, even in their broken and less-than-legitimate-or-legitimating form'. Essentially, there is a fundamental cognitive dissonance at play in contemporary culture: progressive narratives still structure the social and political imaginary, but they are no longer really believed. So even though we are less confident – even incredulous – about the progressive future that the modern child represented, this model of childhood lingers and anxiously co-exists with very different nostalgic associations. Erica Burman articulates these messy, multiple meanings:

> [T]he child as signifier of either the 'true' self, or even the (biographically prior, or never experienced but longed for) 'lost' self, has coincided with a historical sensibility of even greater personal alienation and dislocation. [...] Hence childhood becomes a site for multiple emotional as well as political investments: a repository of hope yet a site of instrumentalisation for the future, but with an equal and opposite nostalgia for the past. (Burman, 2008: 13)

Late twentieth-century socio-economic and cultural change – whether it is conceptualized as post-Fordist, neoliberal and/or postmodern – does not just help produce this overloaded figuration of childhood.[5] Contemporary cultural production also routinely explores these changes through stories and metaphors of childhood, particularly of child abuse. In *Death of a Murderer*, at the very mention of Myra Hindley's name, Billy's wife Sue looks down at the floor and 'seemed to be staring right through the tiles to what lay immediately beneath: the foundations of the house, the dark, damp earth – the end of everything' (*DM*, 9). If the child is a powerful metaphor – however fraught – for both our idealized past and our hopes for a progressive future, child abuse not only damages real children's lives, it destabilizes narratives that are foundational to society, revealing how precarious they really are. Indeed, the trope or metaphor of the abused child articulates the fundamental dissonances that Brown argues define contemporary culture, which may account for the proliferation of cultural narratives about abuse from the late twentieth century onwards. Abused and murdered children like Venetia or Hindley and Brady's victims in *Death of a Murderer* are routinely figured as 'lost in time' (*DM*, 1). They are metaphors for a future that could or should have come to pass but did not; for transformation and development that was violently arrested.

As well as signifying an impossible or precarious future, the figure of the abused child is also increasingly popular as cultural shorthand for exploring a hidden, repressed or traumatically occluded past. This is evident in contemporary novels as diverse as Peace's *Red Riding Quartet* (1999–2002), an explicitly revisionist series of crime novels that present the North of England in the 1970s and 1980s as endemically corrupt and criminal; Hilary Mantel's *Beyond Black* (2005), in which childhood sexual abuse catalyses a medium's ability to communicate with the dead; and Patrick McCabe's *Winterwood* (2006), in which child sexual abuse is the repressed reality of a rural past rapidly becoming an object for nostalgia in an Ireland transformed beyond recognition by neoliberalism. For cultural production that is revisionist and hostile towards a nostalgic view of the recent past like Peace, Mantel and McCabe's fictions, the trope of child sexual abuse represents a logical fit for exploring an abusive historicity. However, a model of the past defined by horror and trauma is not necessarily 'anti-nostalgic' or politically challenging. Rather, it can be another form of nostalgia (from the Greek 'algia'/painful longing for 'nostos'/ home) that positions the past as a stable, determining point of origin, albeit one that is disavowed rather than desired. As Blake Morrison asks in *As If*, his meditation on the James Bulger murder, 'isn't home some place you have as a child, and spend the rest of your time [either] running from or failing to get back to?' (Morrison, 1998: 103).

Roger Luckhurst's work on 'trauma culture' suggests the emergence from the 1990s onwards of a wide-ranging 'articulation of subjectivity [...] organized around the concept of trauma' (Luckhurst, 2003: 28). According to Luckhurst, subjects define themselves in relation to their own trauma, but they also yoke themselves to collective traumas and voyeuristically consume trauma narratives – particularly those of abusive childhoods. Perhaps paradoxically for something defined by its very lack of a 'cohesive narrative, only fragments linked through ominous occlusions', trauma offers a seemingly stable means of self-fashioning (Luckhurst, 2003: 28). As Alison Winter (2012: 179–96) notes, following the memory 'wars' of the 1990s (the debates around the recovered memory/false memory scandals that exemplify the clash between models of memory-as-retrieval and memory-as-dynamic-narrative), the recovery of repressed childhood sexual abuse has become popular shorthand for memorial processes more generally. Middleton and Woods argue that contemporary historical novels present memory rather than historical discourse as the 'superhighway to the past' and that the formal and stylistic strategies through which memory is explored in these texts often reflect historically specific 'collectively shared expectations about how memory works and what it can provide' (Middleton and Woods, 2000: 90–1). These 'shared expectations' of memory are themselves often defined by and also figured through 'traumatic' memories and, more specifically, memories of abuse. In *Death of a Murderer*, Billy's mental and memorial processes are often described using metaphors of water. Memories begin 'floating into his mind', names 'surface' unexpectedly (*DM*, 25). This suggests a psychoanalytically inflected surface/depth model of memory, with 'submerged', hidden or forgotten memories unexpectedly breaking the surface of the subject. *Death of a Murderer* is part of a trend in contemporary writing in which trauma, and particularly child sexual abuse, acts as a trope for a fractured, non-linear historical engagement with a past that is conceived of as simultaneously resistant to narrativization and inescapably determining.

Kincaid argues that too often child abuse offers this totalising explanatory power, it 'explains so much, explains everything. It is the semiotic shorthand that tells us to look no further' (Kincaid, 1998: 12). Burman concurs that conceptions of sexual abuse often represent 'the familiar problem that once the past is seen as the traumatogenic place of origin it is all too easy to conveniently "forget" present day sequelae/causative circumstances' (Burman, 2008: 104). Abuse narratives often suggest models of contemporary subjectivity and historicity being produced and delimited by one 'watershed' event or moment in the past, undermining agency and the capacity for transformation in the present and future. The form that these abuse narratives take, and the ideologies that underpin them, can also be deeply culturally conservative. Kincaid suggests that there is something beguilingly simplistic and attractive about the 'stark moral drama' of paedophilia, with its categories of inherent purity and evil, and that contemporary cultural production uses abuse to tell nostalgic and eschatological narratives of social and moral decline (Kincaid, 1998: 11). Furthermore, the popular presentation of child abusers as highly *individualized* deviant monsters not only isolates their actions from implication in wider social and cultural systems, it 'draws our attention away from [...] structural social problems and away from what may be more pressing pains in our culture' (Kincaid, 1998: 12–13). For Kincaid, these 'structural social problems' are particularly associated with and exacerbated by the neoliberal 'revolution' of the 1980s and beyond, the negative effects of which continue to disproportionately affect children and vulnerable people.

Death of a Murderer does not focus on child sexual abuse in isolation or efface structural social problems, and its figuration of Hindley acknowledges the allure of the simplistic narrative of an 'evil monster' corrupting an otherwise idyllic past but refuses its nostalgic consolation. Indeed, the novel persistently troubles, interrogates and complicates nostalgic investments in childhood and the ways in which nostalgia shapes knowledge-production about the recent past. It questions how and why 'we, through late modernity, cling to [the child] for "nostalgic" groundings' (Jenks, 2005: 112).

Nostalgia and the historical child

The novel's most sustained exploration of the interrelationship between nostalgia and abuse comes from Billy's memories of Trevor Lydgate. During his long overnight shift in the morgue, and despite his attempts 'to push it away' (*DM*, 25) Trevor's name keeps 'surfacing' in Billy's mind until he can 'no longer avoid' remembering: 'it seemed like the name had a voice, and it was calling out to him, demanding his attention' (*DM*, 125). Trevor is an old school friend of Billy's who he encounters unexpectedly in a budget hotel many years later. Over drinks, they discuss their shared childhood:

> 'If you think about it though, we all have to watch our children now, don't we? So many things can happen to them. When we were young, it was different.' He reached for his new pint and took a gulp. 'Back then it was all woods and fields, and we'd be gone for the whole day, and no one even thought twice...' Trevor's voice had started trembling halfway through the sentence, but then it gave out completely, and he put his face in his hands. (*DM*, 129)

Neither Trevor nor the novel can articulate this idyllic, pastoral vision of a 1960s childhood in the face of the darker associations of children being 'gone'. Trevor breaks down and insists that he was abducted by Hindley and Brady, and although he escaped their back bedroom with its bare mattress, camera and pornography, thirty years later he 'felt that he might still be in there':

> What he saw wasn't continuous. It came to him in vivid fragments. Flashes and splinters. As though the film of his life had been slashed to ribbons and then taped back together. He didn't really know how he managed to get away. There were times when he found it impossible to believe. There were times when he thought he must have been in that room for longer, but part of him had shut down, blotting those bits out. There were times when he searched his body for the traces of the things they must have done to him. There were times, too, when he felt that he might still be there, and that all this – he waved a hand to indicate the room, the hotel, and everything outside and beyond – all this was just fantasy or wishful thinking. (*DM*, 137)

Trevor is the paradigmatic abused child in *Death of a Murderer*, and in many ways the paradigmatic trauma-subject. His subjectivity is organized around an experience that he can't quite grasp, articulate or narrativize, and therefore fully 'believe'. The 'film of his life' being splintered and 'slashed to ribbons' suggests both the mechanics of his memorial processes and the coherent narrative presentation of his life story being violently penetrated and damaged, with the metaphor of 'taping back together' suggesting an always fragile and provisional fixity. Trevor is a subject who is brittle and at risk of fraying and fragmentation. He is also 'stuck' in and determined by his traumatic childhood – and as such is figured in liminal and eerily un-adult terms: he has a 'childlike quality', he '[cries] himself to sleep, just as a child might' and his 'legs were smooth and white, and utterly without hair. Somehow this seemed in keeping with the story he had told, the horror he had so narrowly escaped' (*DM*, 141). Trevor Lydgate is defined and inscribed by his abuse: the idea of any space free of its taint or any alternative future is 'fantasy or wishful thinking' (*DM*, 137). Trevor later commits suicide, and at his funeral Billy reminisces about childhood with Trevor's widow: 'He talked about his friendship with Trevor and the adventures they used to have. "Happier days," she said with a weak smile. "Yes", he said. And then added, "For all of us", though he wasn't sure why he'd said that, or what he meant by it' (*DM*, 149–50). Billy's need to propagate the fantasy of 'Happier days' goes beyond consoling a bereaved woman with truisms about childhood. He *needs* to be included within that collective nostalgic fantasy, for reasons that he is unable or unwilling to articulate and interrogate.

It might seem unsurprising that a novel about the Moors Murders complicates a nostalgic fantasy of the recent past. However, as argued above, nostalgia and child sexual abuse are not necessarily opposed. Thinking back to the killings as an adult, Billy 'thought that he remembered' that 'a chill seemed to hang over that part of his childhood, as if, for a while, the sun had been obliterated by dark clouds' (*DM*, 4). A childhood defined as/by sunshine – reminiscent of the nostalgic cliché of endless sunny summer holidays, an idyll never to be repeated in adult life – is 'obliterated' by clouds, but only 'for a while'. This temporary obliteration is organized around a binary opposition: child murders function as the dark mutually constitutive other of the ideology of an unsullied, pure collective childhood. Abuse narratives do not necessarily undermine the Edenic fantasy of 'pure' childhood – in fact, this narrative can be reinforced by the external, adult and asocial threat of the paedophile serpent-in-the-garden. Nevertheless, the crimes' legacies continue to trouble Billy, albeit again in ways that are difficult for him to precisely articulate: 'We were all damaged by what happened, he thought. We were all changed' (*DM*, 155–6). The text's exploration of the indeterminate effects and legacies of the murders is most troublingly played out in Billy's suggestion that Trevor's 'vivid' (*DM*, 137) memories of being abducted by Hindley are actually a traumatic fantasy that masks familial abuse:

> To fall into the clutches of two such dangerous people and yet live to tell the tale. To be lured into that house – actually *into the house* – and then to make a getaway. It sounded like a bizarre fantasy, or a much embroidered version of a far less terrifying event. [...] At some level he thought that what he had heard had all the trappings of a story that

was being told to cover another story, one that had to remain secret. There might well be three stories, then: the story Trevor had told his parents – *I got lost* – the one he told his wife, his brother, and his childhood friend – *I was abducted* – and the one he kept to himself, or even, possibly hid from himself. This third story had never been revealed, probably because it was too close to home, perhaps it even involved members of his family. The advantage of the version he had told Billy was that it allowed him to unburden himself without actually giving anything away. (*DM*, 154–5)

That Trevor experienced some kind of trauma is not in doubt, but the 'truth' of those events is not locatable for Billy and is never revealed in the text. In *Death of a Murderer*, stories about childhood are never straightforward or stable sources of knowledge. One kind of story functions to cover up another story or multiple stories. In this case, Billy suspects that the public horrors of the Moors Murders gave Trevor a form through which he could express something half-understood or half-remembered about his own childhood: 'If Billy's theory was correct, it showed how deeply that series of murders had embedded itself in the nation's psyche. No one who was alive at the time could ever be entirely free of it' (*DM*, 155). In many senses, Trevor's story functions as a metonym for the novel's own approach to the Moors Murders: it is a murky prism through which constitutive cultural narratives about childhood are troubled and denaturalized. Nostalgia, which Jenks argues is the dominant contemporary mode for understanding childhood, is exposed as an illusory adult projection, which has toxic effects for children. Trevor cannot tell his parents about his abusive experience because it would shatter *their* innocent ideas about childhood: 'When he saw them drive up in the car, he thought how innocent they looked. It was as if he was the parent and they were the children. He felt they needed to be protected' (*DM*, 138). Nostalgia is structured by mutual repression: the fantasy must be maintained by and for adults, and children like Trevor suffer to maintain it.

And yet a nostalgic retro-memory of childhood in the sunny 1960s is not replaced by an equally simplistic indictment of the period.[6] *Death of a Murderer* resists the popular association between the Moors

Murders and the permissive politics of the Wilson years, which is still being lazily peddled in cultural histories of the decade (Sandbrook, 2007: 570–1). The novel acknowledges the desire to understand why Hindley – who unlike Brady, was not judged to be mentally ill – was involved in these iconic crimes, but does not – indeed, cannot – provide easy answers. Billy finds himself on Saddleworth Moor, where the remains of victim Keith Bennett still remain undiscovered, and wanders the disorientating, 'treeless and primitive' landscape, secretly hoping for 'a miraculous discovery' (DM: 26, 28):

> Once again, he had the feeling that there was something to be discovered, but it was like having a word on the tip of your tongue and knowing you would never remember it. There were things here that couldn't be squared away – not by him in any case. He stared off into a gully, imagining a man leading a small boy by the hand. After a minute, only the man's head and shoulders showed above the bank, and the boy wasn't visible at all … The snow had blown in from the East the night before, and it was coming again, the air closing in, surrounding him, a whirl of tiny flakes. He turned and started back towards the car. (DM, 29)

The text foregrounds the desire to discover not only Bennett's body but recover knowledge that will make these crimes explicable and again bring into focus something that Billy is seemingly unable to articulate about his own life. However, the buried and hidden 'truth' Billy seeks to discover in the crimes is as impenetrable as the frozen landscape and the forbidding weather. Even Billy's imagination fails him as the man and boy, presumably representing Brady and Bennett, are rapidly obscured. Nostalgia involves – as well as its solipsistic and sentimental associations – a longing for fixity, stability and explication that positions the past as a knowable point of origin, whether disavowed or desired. Death of a Murderer acknowledges that desire, but refuses or is unable to explain or historicize the past in a way that emphasizes causality.

In a similar way, the text complicates the comforting figuration of the child abuser as a monstrous other. Instead, the figure of the abuser is deployed to interrogate the uneasy investments we have in the figure of the child. When Billy violently confronts Venetia's father, he is disturbed by how ordinary he is: 'he had imagined a deviant, a pervert, someone who stood out from the rest of society, but this old man not only resembles any other old man you might see on the street, he also resembled his daughter' (*DM*, 210–11). Billy's queasiness regarding this imbrication of adult and child, abuser and victim is also evident in his interactions with Hindley:

> He tried to imagine the woman as a little girl, but it made him feel uncomfortable. It was as if he were placing her on the same footing as her victims; it seemed insensitive at best, at worst a kind of violation. Yet there must have been a time, mustn't there, when she was innocent? People didn't want to think about that of course. There was one image of her in the popular mind – the dyed-blonde hair, the brooding gaze – and that was it. There was no before, no after. [...] And as he sat there at the table it suddenly occurred to him that he had never seen a picture of her as a child, not even one. Didn't her mother have any? If not, what had happened to them? Had they been suppressed? Destroyed? It was a strange absence, unsettling, almost unjust, though he thought he understood the need for it. (*DM*, 180–1)

Billy understands that there is a 'need' for Hindley to stand outside the fundamental category of 'the child', because dominant cultural understandings of childhood as an inherently 'innocent' time cannot withstand her incorporation. Abusers like Hindley constitute 'childhood' by being its aberrant opposite: monstrous others who, through their abuse, subvert everything childhood stands for in contemporary culture: purity, futurity, safety, home. Yet, as Billy's realization makes clear, Hindley manifestly was a child too; she did not arrive as a fully formed 'monster'. Perhaps her own brutal childhood laid the foundation for her crimes and the sadomasochistic, abusive relationship with Brady. The novel explores those possibilities in Hindley's dialogues with Billy. The figure of a 'frail, dark-haired boy of about thirteen' wearing a 'pair of black swimming-trunks, and his body [...] the colour of cement' (*DM*, 123) appears alongside Hindley at one point, the spectre of Hindley's drowned childhood friend. Did his death traumatize her? Might that have been the turning-point? The text resists easy answers: Hindley's spectre is slippery and impossible to pin down. What *is* clear is that the text identifies a desperate need to maintain the hermetically sealed figure of the 'pure' child: any alternative or more complicated perspective must be 'suppressed' or 'destroyed' like the missing images of Hindley as anything other than her iconic mug shot: 'the features individually too familiar by now to be read as an integrated, blood warmed face. As usual, Hindley looks like a composite, an identikit, a media emanation, a hypothetical who never existed in the flesh' (Burn, 1991: 100). Adults often have too much invested in the nostalgic stories we tell *through* 'childhood', including stories of sexual abuse, to easily tolerate their complication.

However, as this chapter has argued, *Death of a Murderer* does complicate these nostalgic narratives. What is more, nostalgia is revealed to elide the complexity of supposedly 'ordinary' children's experiences. Billy's relationship with his childhood best friend Raymond is not innocent; it has distinctly queer and sadomasochistic undercurrents: 'there was something driven about Raymond, something merciless' (*DM*, 60). There are parallels between Hindley's supposed manipulation at the hands of Brady and Billy's passivity and desire. As she slyly points out: '"You did everything he said." She lit another cigarette. She took her time. "You were so *obedient*. Even dogs aren't that obedient."' (*DM*, 183). However, Billy's relationship with Raymond is more than just a neat metaphor for Hindley and Brady's. It is much more difficult to pin down: exhilarating, anxious, dangerous and joyful, simultaneously 'something so exciting [...] and something he wished he hadn't been part of, something he would rather have forgotten' (*DM*, 69). Like Trevor Lydgate and Myra Hindley, Billy's childhood exceeds and undermines nostalgic categorization, and forces critical engagement with the stories we tell about 'childhood'.

Precarious futures

As well as interrogating different forms of nostalgia, *Death of a Murderer* also destabilizes the second constitutive cultural investment in childhood: the pervasive idea that 'the child' is an uncomplicated symbol of progress, possibility and futurity. Throughout the novel, a remarkable pattern emerges in which all children face uncertain and precarious futures – victims of sexual abuse or child abduction like Trevor, and the haunted, binge-drinking Venetia, are only the most extreme examples of subjects unable to move beyond blighted and determining childhoods. Billy's job as a policeman puts him into contact with a wide range of dysfunctional families, and he and his colleagues see their job as little more than 'dealing with rubbish that no one else wanted to deal with. Most of them had gone into the job with good intentions, thinking they could be of use, but they soon realized that the task was well nigh impossible' (*DM*, 91); 'In all his time as a police officer, there were only one or two teenagers whose lives he could honestly claim to have changed for the better' (*DM*, 69). This lack of faith in the possibility of progress is reflected in a model of the next generation ineluctably repeating the actions of their parents: 'Recently a constable in his fifties had told Billy that he was now arresting the sons and grandsons of people he had arrested when he first started out. The crime figures might go up or down, but nothing changed, not really' (*DM*, 93). Missing teenager Rebecca Williams, who Billy fears is the victim of violence at home, is another example: 'the look [she] had in the photograph still haunted him. *I've tried,* her face seemed to be saying, *I really have, but it's no use*' (*DM*, 92). Billy is depressed by this socio-economic determinism, and the realization that he can do nothing to intervene and challenge the lack of 'possibilities' Rebecca is stuck with, and the kind of limited future she seems doomed to inhabit. Her photograph may not be 'old-fashioned, ham-fisted black-and-white' like the 'little faces' of Brady and Hindley's victims reproduced in the tabloids, but she too is a 'victim' (*DM*, 3). Further, seemingly random and inexplicable symbols of arrested development focalized through the figure of the child punctuate the text. Billy recalls attending the crime scene where 'a dead baby had been found at the bottom of a bed' (*DM*, 95). His memories of the suicide of Shena Coates, who performs a certain kind of feminine future at the same time as she rejects it, are perhaps most haunting of all:

> She was wearing a velvet dress and a pair of high heels, and [...]
> locked herself in the garden shed, applied lipstick, rouge, eye-shadow
> and mascara herself, and then hanged herself. She was eleven years
> old. You could still see her handprints on the window where she had
> tried to clean the glass. She had needed more light, in order to do her
> makeup properly. (*DM*, 24–5)

Taken individually, these children are tragic or violent anomalies. But
together, they form a pattern that defines childhood as either something you do not survive, or that traps you in an uncertain and inescapably precarious future.

Yet, as this chapter has argued, childhood is inextricably bound up
with futurity in the contemporary cultural and political imaginary.
When Billy and Sue move to Ipswich, Sue feels 'a kind of restless-
ness or hollowness, the sense that she hadn't fully occupied the space
around her. The space inside her too, [...] she'd had a miscarriage
and she was frightened she might not be able to have children. Words
like "security" and "the future" crept into her conversation' (*DM*, 35).
When Billy proposes marriage 'a dreamy smile rose on to her face,
as if he'd reminded her of something a long time ago, in her childhood' (*DM*, 36). The multiple temporalities invested in the figure of
child in this quotation are suggestive: marriage, with its promises of
'security' and 'future', rooted for Sue in dreams of childhood, in the
double sense of her own past and her future child. Sue sees pregnancy
as a way of 'securing' the future and 'occupying' the world. And eventually they do have a bossy, brilliant daughter – Emma, who is born
with Down's Syndrome. Her genetic disorder leaves her vulnerable,
needing constant monitoring, and with a terrifying propensity to
disappear. Exhausted and depressed on a cliff-side walk in Whitby,
Sue even fleetingly considers killing her: 'She stood in her daughter's
shadow, and she came so close to reaching out that her hands seemed
to throb' (*DM*, 85). Rather than security, Emma symbolizes 'the fragility of things. Their life together. Their foothold in the world' (*DM*,
86).

By the end of *Death of a Murderer*, Billy is able to cathartically
slough off the presence of Hindley in the morgue, which seems to

tentatively offer the promise of progress. However, the novel ends in a much more ambivalent way with Billy bathing his daughter and questioning Emma's future:

> He had wondered then what would become of her. What would he and Sue decide to do about her future? Would she always live at home, with them? Who would care for her when they were dead? Or would she, with her damaged heart, die first? (*DM*, 249–50)

The novel's destabilization of Burman's definition of childhood as a 'repository of hope' through its pattern of abused, fragile or dead children is further emphasized in these final pages (Burman, 2008: 13). In *Death of a Murderer*, '[t]hings like that were always happening, it seemed, or on the point of happening' (*DM*, 225). Childhood becomes a metaphor not for progress and possibility, but for a lack of confidence in our unstable, stratified present, and an uncertain, precarious collective future.

Conclusion

In his final dialogue with Hindley, Billy concludes that the public hated her not only for her crimes but because she 'had reminded them of a truth that they had overlooked, or hidden from, or lied to themselves about' (*DM*, 198). The 'truth' is that childhood is more complex, more threatened and more threatening than we can often stand to acknowledge, and that the stories we tell about it are inadequate, even obfuscatory. Those constitutive cultural narratives act, in Edelman's (2004: 31) words, as a 'disciplinary image' that limits discourse and our social and political horizons. Child abuse – a threat not only to real children's lives, but to cultural investments in childhood – highlights our anxieties about childhood, and by association pastness, society and the shape of our collective future. But the stories we tell about abuse are often conservative, and simplistic – affirming structuring definitions and assumptions about 'childhood' through the figure of a monstrous external threat. By contrast, *Death of a Murderer* uses metaphors of child abuse to interrogate and undermine these stories and others – the neat narratives of nostalgia and futurity or the clear schema of the post-modern and the modern child. The novel presents the Moors Murders as not simply an aberrant event, but a brutal example of an underlying logic or social system in which children – and what the figures of the child and childhood *represent* – are insecure and unsafe. That logic is never systematized or clearly explained, but Thomson's novel disquietingly forces readers and critics to question what is 'overlooked, or hidden [...] or lied [...] about' (*DM*, 198) in contemporary attachments to childhood.

Notes

1 As is often the case in Thomson's work, *Death of a Murderer* is defined by claustrophobia and stasis: 'The air seemed taut, almost rigid, as if the entire hospital had taken a breath in the early hours of Friday morning and was still holding it.' (*DM*, 15) This pregnant pause both contributes to and contrasts with the lack of control Billy feels over the non-linear memories that trouble and disorientate him: 'He felt unsteady, giddy. He felt as if the world was accelerating away from him in all directions. At the same time, everything had remained exactly where it was.' (*DM*, 119)

2 The 'Moors Murders' is the label popularly given to the murders of five children carried out between 1963 and 1965 around Greater Manchester by Ian Brady and Myra Hindley, some of whom were buried on Saddleworth Moor, to the East of the city. The extent of Hindley's involvement in the torture and killing of their victims is contested, and is a question that drives the conversations between Hindley's revenant and Billy in *Death of a Murderer.*

3 Following revelations about the crimes of Jimmy Savile, Operation Yewtree was launched by the Metropolitan Police (BBC News, 2012). Initially focusing on Savile, the enquiry later broadened its focus to include other alleged abusers, primarily celebrities and those in the entertainment industry. Operation Hydrant, a wide-ranging national investigation into 'historic' child sex offences was later launched (Laville, 2015). Controversial allegations of paedophillia have circulated about the late Prime Minister Sir Edward Heath and former Home Secretary Leon Brittan, as well as various other high profile politicians and civil servants. Some of these enquiries have since been abandoned. For journalistic accounts of paedophilia see Bob Long and DCI Bob McLachlan (2002) *The Hunt for Britain's Paedophiles* (London: Hodder and Stoughton); and

Jon Silverman and David Wilson (2002) *Innocence Betrayed: Paedophilia, the Media and Society* (Cambridge: Polity Press). One of the most popular cultural forms child abuse narratives take comes from 'misery memoirs' such as Sophie Young with Linda Watson Brown (2013) *Please will someone help me?* (London: Penguin). Examples of child sexual abuse narratives on television and film include *Care* (BBC, 2001), *Broadchurch* (ITV, 2013), *This is England '86* (Channel 4, 2010), *The Missing* (BBC, 2014), *Eastenders* (BBC, 2001, 2008), *Red Riding Trilogy* (Channel 4, 2009). The BBC crime drama *Line of Duty*, which focuses on an internal police anti-corruption squad, took elite involvement and conspiracy in child sexual exploitation as the focus of its third series in 2016. Each series the conspiracy is revealed to be more complex and further embedded in powerful institutions, and therefore this series. Following previous storylines involving drug dealing and gangland murders, this focus on sexual abuse in some ways represents a logical escalation: in twenty-first-century culture, as one character puts it, child sexual abuse and collusion between authorities and abusers represents society's 'darkest secret.' Some further examples from contemporary fiction will be explored during the course of this chapter.

4 One example of the way in which narratives of child abuse can elide complex questions and problematics is Denise Mina's crime novel *The Field of Blood* (2005), which transposes the James Bulger murder from Liverpool in the 1990s to Glasgow in the early 1980s. Its procedural narrative uncovers the adult influences that (in this novel, literally) drove two children to murder another, simultaneously rendering this fictional version of a real murder more palatable and 'understandable', and emphasising the social context – notably post-industrial poverty and deprivation – that helped to warp two ten-year-old murderers. However, when child sex abuse is revealed as a key factor in the case/narrative, it actually acts to efface these social and contextual factors, rendering a crime with complex social and political provenances the sole result of individual deviance, and resolving the 'faultline narrative' generated by this child murder.

5 Svetlana Boym (2001: 3–32) influentially argues that nostalgia, which emerges as a concept in seventeenth-century Europe, is a reaction against the spatial-temporal transformations and progressive metanarratives of modernity.

6 See Vardy (2015) for the argument that commercialized retro-memory of a lost and less complicated past often manifests itself through an idealized focus on childhood and an object-oriented historiography.

Works Cited

BBC News (2012) 'Jimmy Savile abuse claims: Police pursue 120 lines of enquiry', 9 October, URL (consulted 26 July 2016): http://www.bbc.co.uk/news/uk-19887019

Boym, Svetlana (2001) *The Future of Nostalgia*. New York: Basic Books.

Brown, Wendy (2001) *Politics Out of History*. Princeton, NJ: Princeton University Press.

Burman, Erica (2008) *Developments: Child, Image, Nation*. London: Routledge.

Burn, Gordon (1991) *Alma Cogan*. London: Minerva.

Caselli, Daniela (2010) 'Kindergarten Theory: Childhood, Affect, Critical Thought', *Feminist Theory* 11(3): 241–54.

Eaglestone, Robert (2013)' *Contemporary Fiction: A Very Short Introduction*. Oxford: Oxford University.

Edelman, Lee (2004) *No Future: Queer Theory and the Death Drive*. Durham: Duke University Press.

Jenks, Chris (2005) *Childhood*, 2nd edn. Abingdon: Routledge.

Kincaid, James R. (1998) *Erotic Innocence: The Culture of Child Molesting*. Durham, NC: Duke University Press.

Laville, Sandra (2015) '1400 investigated in child sex abuse inquiry, including politicians', *Guardian*, 20 May, URL (consulted June 2015): http://www.theguardian.com/uk-news/2015/may/20/1400-suspects-operation-hydrant-politician-and-celebrity-child-sex-abuse-inquiry

Luckhurst, Roger (2003) 'Traumaculture', *New Formations* 50: 28–47.

McCabe, Patrick (2007) *Winterwood*. London: Bloomsbury.

Mantel, Hilary (2010) *Beyond Black*. London: Fourth Estate.

Middleton, Peter and Tim Woods (2000) *Literatures of Memory*. Manchester: Manchester University Press.

Mina, Denise (2005) *The Field of Blood*. London: Orion.

Morrison, Blake (1998) *As If*. London: Granta.

Peace, David (1999) *Nineteen Seventy Four*. London: Serpent's Tail.

Peace, David (2002) *Nineteen Eighty Three*. London: Serpent's Tail.

Rose, Jacqueline (1993) *The Case of Peter Pan, or The Impossibility of Children's Fiction*. Philadelphia: University of Pennsylvania Press.

Sandbrook, D. (2007) *White Heat: A History of Britain in the Swinging Sixties.* London: Abacus.

Vardy, C. (2015) 'Remembering the 1980s in David Mitchell's *Black Swan Green*', in Leggett, B. and Venezia, A. (eds) *Twenty-first-century British Fiction.* Canterbury: Gylphi.

Winter, A. (2012) *Memory: Fragments of a Modern History.* Chicago, IL: University of Chicago Press.

THE GHOSTLY PRESENCE OF HER
REPRESENTATIONS OF MYRA HINDLEY
IN *DEATH OF A MURDERER*

Rhona Gordon

The events in Rupert Thomson's novel *Death of a Murderer* (2007) centre around policeman Billy Tyler's twelve-hour nightshift guarding Myra Hindley's body in the hospital morgue. In the quiet of the night the appearance of Hindley's ghost prompts Billy to (re)consider his life to date. The novel intersperses present, linear events with snapshots of Billy's past, focusing on key relationships that have influenced his path. This chapter will consider representations of Hindley's ghost in the novel and will argue that as well as propelling the events of the novel, the figure of the ghost also considers the nature of evil and brings into focus questions about the relationship between public and private memory.

The real Myra Hindley died on 15 November 2002, aged 60, in West Sussex Hospital at Bury St. Edmunds while serving a life sentence for the sexual abuse, torture and murder of three children, crimes she carried out with her partner Ian Brady. Hindley and Brady murdered at least five children between July 1963 and October 1965 and three of the victims' bodies were found buried on Saddleworth Moor. The horrific details of their crimes have ensured that the Moors Murders have never lost their power to shock. Even at the beginning of the twenty-first century her death evoked strong emotions with various newspaper headlines on Hindley's death proclaiming her the 'Moors monster' (Sapsted and Bunyan, 2002) and 'evil' (*Sun*, 2002). The opening page of *Death of a Murderer* acknowledges this media outrage: 'It had all happened years ago, in the sixties, but people had never forgiven her for what she had done. Never forgiven, and never forgotten' (*DM*, 1). Indeed, one reason why the Moors Murders are so prominent in public consciousness is because the final missing body, that of twelve-year-old Keith Bennett, has never been recovered, and it is believed Ian Brady is withholding vital information on his burial site on the Moor (*BBC News*, 2012).

Fact vs. fiction

Death of a Murderer takes the real-life death of Myra Hindley and imagines what it would be like for someone to guard her dead body, and the effect this might have on those involved. This mixture of fact and fiction, sometimes known as 'faction', has been utilized frequently in the early twenty-first century by writers such as Gordon Burn, David Peace and Andrew O'Hagan, alongside Thomson. Faction explores the historical figure's moment in time and seeks to understand them or their circumstances from different perspectives. In her study of the texts of David Peace, Katy Shaw examines Peace's blending of fact and fiction in, amongst other works, *The Red Riding Quartet* (1999–2002) and *GB84* (2004), and argues that his work offers an analysis of the modern world and an attempt to understand the past:

> In Peace's novels the past is not comprised of hard facts but a great number of knowable histories, invented, overlooked, destroyed, denied or disregarded. Sourced in a belief that 'fiction can illuminate a time and a place more clearly than fact', the value of Peace's fiction comes from its celebration of plurality and lack of conclusions. (Shaw, 2011: 3)

Providing a space in which to imagine past events is also crucial in *Death of a Murderer*. As will be discussed below, the appearance of Hindley's ghost questions the mediatized version of Hindley that has become most widely known. To mix fact with fiction is not a recent development in the history of the novel and Linda Hutcheon has labelled the interweaving of fiction and historical fact 'historiographic metafiction', arguing that,

> the novel has always been inherently ambivalent since its inception: it has always been both fictional and worldly. If this is so, then postmodern historiographic metafiction merely foregrounds this inherent paradox by having its historical and socio-political groundings sit uneasily alongside its self-reflexivity (Hutcheon, 1989: 14).

Postmodern novels such as *Death of a Murderer*, then, differ from earlier novels by drawing attention to their characters' fictiveness and providing equal space for the fictive and factual to interact. This leads to history being consumed in a certain way. In considering how fiction and fact relate to each other in the novel, Fredric Jameson examines the novels of E. L. Doctorow and argues the mix of history and fiction, as opposed to 'pure' historical novels, means that the reader is required to know what is fact and what is fiction in order to fully understand the mechanisms underlying the novel, and as a result, '[t]he historical novel can no longer set out to represent the historical past; it can only "represent" our ideas and stereotypes about the past (which thereby at once becomes "pop history")' (Jameson, 1991: 25). Faction is interested in the ways in which history is packaged and consumed rather than a straight re-telling of the past. Indeed, *Death of a Murderer* does not go into great detail about Hindley's crimes and does not mention her by name. While the novel can be read without prior knowledge, for those who know of Hindley and Brady's crimes the narrative is unquestionably about them. The novel does not seek to instruct, but to question our perceptions and previous knowledge.

The uncanny spectre

Hindley's ghost first appears in the trees outside the hospital, her cigarette burning in the dark, and her first words are almost jarringly mundane: 'It wasn't that dramatic', and 'Do you like my suit? I got it from a catalogue' (*DM*, 106). Perhaps more is expected from our monsters – not for them to comment on their clothing. Throughout the text

Thomson undercuts the idea of what it means to be evil and how evil should be represented. The horrible familiarity and ordinariness of this figure recalls Freud's theory of the uncanny. For Freud, ghosts are the 'most potent' (Freud, 2003: 148) examples of the uncanny. Uncanny, translated from the German for *unheimlich* (unhomely), is that which 'belongs to the realm of the frightening, of what evokes fear and dread' (Freud, 2003: 123) and more specifically: 'the uncanny is that species of the frightening that goes back to what was once well known and had long been familiar' (Freud, 2003: 124). Hindley's ghost affirms both of these states as she evokes a sense of dread and is all too familiar. Billy notes on hearing her voice: 'A Manchester accent – even after all these years' (*DM*, 106). The familiar accent reminds Billy of the Hindley of the past and she is instantly recognizable. However, the ghost does not just appear in the hospital grounds. On route to the Moors, Billy passes a car going in the other direction with a familiar-looking driver: 'The driver was a woman with blonde hair, the top half of her face hidden by a lowered sunshield. Only the blunt curve of her chin was visible, and a hard mouth made even harder by her bright-red lipstick' (*DM*, 27). Hindley's face appears not just in bodily or ghostly form but in passers-by, suggesting that she cannot be contained: she is literally everywhere and has the potential to reappear, like a virus. Her potential to reappear thus emphasizes the horror which lurks in the mundane.

The appearance of the ghost signals that the novel is a hauntological text, or a text concerned with haunting. The term 'hauntology' comes from Jacques Derrida's *Spectres of Marx* (1994: xix) in which he discusses the ghost that appears to Hamlet and notes: 'Furtive and untimely, the apparition of the spectre does not belong to that time, it does not give time'. According to Derrida, ghosts are not located in a temporal dimension, and Hindley straddles different times throughout the novel, haunting both Billy's past and present. Derrida (1994: xx) goes on to argue that spectres appear in order to draw attention to unresolved issues and that 'one must reckon with them'. And reckon with Hindley Billy does, or at least he tries to. Hindley's appearance prompts a shaken Billy to consider his own ghosts, as he still carries with him the memories of past relationships, including his ex-girlfriend Venetia, his school friend Raymond Percival and his father: memories that he is not yet able to fully consign to the past. The ghost of Hindley appears several times throughout the night of his shift and prompts Billy to ask her questions. He wonders: 'Had the woman known what effect she had on those around her? What would it be like to know that?' (*DM*, 74). Frustratingly she vanishes before giving any answers and does not provide Billy with the closure for which he is looking. Whilst denying the reader insight into Hindley's own inner life, the ghost does not allow Billy's inner life to go unexamined and at times enjoys his discomfort: 'He could feel her watching him to see what he would do next. She was feasting on his embarrassment, his shame' (*DM*, 183). This exchange perhaps displays the ghost's cruel streak, yet as this is told from Billy's viewpoint, the interpretation is highly subjective. It is not clear whether the ghost is taunting him or whether Billy is projecting his own self-consciousness onto the spectre.

Mark Fisher's *Ghosts of My Life* (2014) discusses the prevalence of ghosts and haunted spaces, systems and art forms in early twentieth-century life and applies and develops Derrida's concept of hauntology in his cultural criticism. For Fisher, hauntology does not need to contain ghosts, he proposes 'to think of hauntology as *the agency of the virtual*, with the spectre understood not as anything supernatural, but that which acts without (physically) existing' (Fisher, 2014: 18). In terms of Thomson's novel, it is useful to think of hauntology as relating to both being haunted by a spectre and to events of the past. Fisher describes two directions in hauntology based on Martin Hägglund's distinction between 'the *no longer* and *the not yet*' (Fisher, 2014: 19). These are:

> that which is (in actuality is) *no longer*, but which *remains* effective as a virtuality (the traumatic 'compulsion to repeat', a fatal pattern). The second sense of hauntology refers to that which (in actuality) has *not yet* happened, but which is *already* effective in the virtual (an attraction in an anticipation shaping current behaviour). (Fisher, 2014: 19)

Death of a Murderer fits into this first description: Hindley no longer exists but remains effective as a malignant presence reliving past events and forcing Billy to relive key moments in his own life, such as his brief intense relationship with his former childhood friend Raymond. After a short break outside the hospital during which he sees Hindley's ghost, their conversation prompts a shaken Billy to phone his friend Neil: 'Neil had given the encouragement he needed without even being asked. Friends could do that' (*DM*, 109). Yet when Billy returns inside, the unsettling presence of Hindley makes him think of an alternative scenario – the possibility that friends, rather than offering encouragement and comfort, can offer encouragement to become involved in darker activities. On returning to the hospital and eating his sandwich, Billy recalls a holiday he took with Raymond when they were both teenagers. After running out of money Billy asks Raymond for some cash to buy food. Refusing to give Billy any, a fight breaks out whereupon Raymond calls out 'Thief!' to attract passers-by and embarrass Billy (*DM*, 115). This uncomfortable event, following on from Raymond controlling their supplies and denying Billy sufficient food, shows Billy that the friend he thought he had is in fact a stranger: 'in that moment he had the feeling that he didn't know Raymond at all, that the two of them had never met before, and that he had, in fact attacked and robbed a total stranger' (*DM*, 115). This disturbing episode suggests that even people who are considered friends still have the capacity to surprise. Even though the event happened long ago, it still has the power to shock and again highlights the danger that lurks in everyday, seemingly mundane, life.

Throughout the text there are repeated references to the fluidity of, or the thin boundary between, life, death, past, present, reality and invention. This fluidity and fragility is evident in the figuration of Billy's body: 'The inside of his head felt hollow, scooped out, smooth as an empty shell' (*DM*, 26). Billy's wife Sue is aware of the 'fragility of things': 'The wall protecting them was so very thin. In fact it was a miracle that it had held for as long as it had' (*DM*, 87). This observation contains the threat of disaster erupting at any time and tearing Billy and his family's lives apart. Throughout the novel there is a sense of instability and of worlds always on the verge of collapse. Hindley's ghost, too, is a totem of a porous world with malevolent forces always at its edges, threatening to break in. Alongside this unspecified threat is also the sense of unreality in day-to-day life as everyday milestones are shown to be potentially meaningless. Billy and Sue seem to have a good life: 'they had more or less everything they were supposed to have – a house, a child, a car, a job, a pension – but nothing felt secure at all, and nothing felt quite real either' (*DM*, 48). Against the backdrop of domesticity it is revealed that Billy has had an extra-marital affair and that both Billy and Sue have struggled with their daughter Emma's Downs Syndrome. It is within this unstable world that Billy sees Hindley's ghost.

Dangerous bodies

Even after her death, attempts are made to control Hindley's presence: Billy's job on the night in question is to ensure peace before Hindley's burial. 'We have to make sure nothing happens' (*DM*, 18), his superior officer instructs. Billy is to protect the body from those who would like to do it harm, however there is always the suggestion that he is protecting the outside world from the body. Like Samuel Beckett's *Waiting for Godot* (1953), this is a text where, in one sense, nothing much happens. Billy feels as if he is guarding an absence, it is as if 'he was guarding a phantom, or a figment of somebody's imagination' (*DM*, 66). In actuality, efforts were made to erase Hindley's presence after her death and Carol Ann Lee describes how everything in Hindley's hospital room was incinerated after she died:

> A spokesman told the press that the hospital administration was sensitive to future patients and therefore 'the room has been cleared of everything that was used during her care and has been redecorated.' The smell of fresh paint drifted down the corridor, but not as far as the mortuary, where Myra lay isolated from the other dead and under police guard. (Lee, 2010: 19)

Thomson considers these details and describes how efforts are made by the mortuary staff to erase any trace of Hindley, so that her bedding is burnt as 'non-chemical waste' (*DM*, 20) – ostensibly to stop any souvenir hunters, but the incineration also raises the question of who would want to obtain those sheets. Sue fears that Hindley's evil will be able to permeate their home through Billy: 'It's not healthy to be close to something like that' (*DM*, 7). Something, it is notable, not someone. This is in contrast to the tabloids, and the souvenir hunters, who want to 'sense the power, the horror. They wanted a direct line to the unknown' (*DM*, 13). This is not a unique phenomenon and we are reminded of events such as the demolition of Fred and Rosemary West's house at 25 Cromwell House after their imprisonment to stop souvenir hunters, and the tourists who still pass by the former home of Yorkshire Ripper Peter Sutcliffe.

Death of a Murderer denies the reader a direct line to Hindley and does not detail any of her crimes or sensationalize her life. Indeed, though she haunts the novel, Hindley is never named and she is always 'She'. This woman with unnatural powers recalls H. Rider Haggard's *She* (1887) in that She is both worldly and other-worldly. 'She-who-must-be-obeyed' is the Queen of a lost African city who possesses supernatural powers including the ability to heal wounds and read minds. She is thousands of years old, seemingly immortal, and her beauty has the ability to enchant men and beguile her followers. The powers She possesses cannot be rationally explained and this mirrors how Hindley is viewed: as a malignant force, an aberration who has committed awful crimes that cannot be fully explained, even years after they were committed.

The image of evil

The ordinary, unremarkable appearance of Hindley's ghost stands in stark contrast to the iconic mugshot which has become firmly lodged in public consciousness in the years following her arrest and imprisonment. With its cool-eyed stare and blonde beehive the image is instantly recognizable and has become synonymous with Hindley's evil acts. Yet the normality of the ghost in Thomson's novel upsets this idea of recognizable evil and calls into question the nature of evil. *Myra* (1995) by Marcus Harvey uses children's handprints to create a black and white mosaic of Hindley's police mugshot, taken after her arrest in 1965. Controversial when it was first exhibited, and still controversial now (as demonstrated by the 2008 Beijing Olympics controversy where images of Hindley were used in a promotional video for the London 2012 Olympics), the painting comments on the power of Hindley's image created by over thirty years of media interest and the contrast between adult evil and childhood innocence. By stripping the image back to its constituent parts with the black and white pixels of the photograph equated to the handprints of children, the power of Harvey's painting is in reminding the viewer that actual crimes were committed – real children were hurt by a real woman (and man). The painting is not just an iconic image: it is the marker of a historical event and the children's handprints refocus the horror of the image. The painting also suggests the particular gender dynamic that drives so much of the hatred against Hindley, that a woman could hurt children is a particularly uncomfortable idea and her acts have made her a demon, a monstrous anti-mother.

Hindley was in many ways defined by her image, for the public there was no other Myra except the one offered by the photograph. In *Death of a Murderer* Thomson comments on the infamous police photo:

> There she was, perfectly preserved, despite the thirty-six years she had spent behind bars: the sixties beehive hairdo, the sullen, bruised-looking mouth and, most potent of all, that steady black stare, so full of defiance and hostility, so empty of regret. (*DM*, 3)

Time has not diminished the public's perception of Hindley and the photograph undermines any restorative work that may have taken place during her prison sentence, as with the power of the photo comes the end of Hindley's story as Thomson writes: 'There was one image of her in the popular mind – the dyed-blonde hair, the brooding gaze – and that was it. There was no before, no after. No childhood, and no old age' (*DM*, 181). Thomson examines the realities of Hindley's life, she is not just a bee-hived monster, but a real woman with a life that did not start with her arrest and end with her imprisonment. Both Harvey and Thomson deconstruct the popular image so that Hindley is complicated, rather than reduced, by the sum of her parts. The image and cultural afterlife of Myra Hindley are also

explored by Gordon Burn in his novel *Alma Cogan* (1991) and she re-
appears in several of Burn's pieces written for British broadsheets. In
his article exploring the 1997 Young British Artist exhibition, Sensation, where *Myra* was first put on display, Burn describes the outraged
reaction to Harvey's painting and the popular belief that evil can be
captured by a photograph:

> It is the belief that it is the terribleness of her 'inner being' that can be
> plainly etched on the thirty-year-old police mugshot of Hindley [...]
> In the sixteenth century, Protestant iconoclasts believed that evil in-
> fluences could come into the body through the eyes and corrupt the
> viewer. And the events of recent weeks have shown that it is still pos-
> sible to hold these views, four hundred years later. (Burn, 2009: 391)

This idea that someone can be identified as evil, merely by their appearance, is both unsettling and comforting as it means that the malevolent perpetrator could appear anywhere, and be anyone yet, they
can be easily identified and placed within an understandable narrative. Evil, it is suggested, cannot be simply contained and threatens to
seep out and contaminate the viewer: just to be in the presence of evil
is dangerous and a potential threat to healthy bodies and minds. Yet if
evil is able to be identified then, it is implied, its threat can be guarded
against. Thomson investigates this uncanny idea of the signifiers of
evil throughout his novel, and *Death of a Murderer* is concerned with
Hindley's body not just as a media construct but in its corporeal form,
as a physical entity that was once alive, and in its subsequent ghostly
figuration. Thomson's use of the uncanny undermines the comforting
idea that evil can be read on an individual's face or identified easily.

Indeed, in *Death of a Murderer* the policewoman guarding Hindley
towards the end of her life notes that if someone were not to know
who Hindley was, and were not aware of her murderous past, 'You
would've thought she was normal' (*DM*, 227). It is this lack of distinction between murderer and normal human emotions and behaviour
that Thomson is interested in exploring, and it is through Hindley's
ghostly presence that the complexities of her case are tested. Thomson undermines the oddly cosy idea that child-murderers are uncomplicated monsters who can be identified and guarded against. Hind-

ley's life in prison is at odds with her monstrous public image, as Lee notes in her biography:

> It is an unbearable fact that Myra Hindley was capable of love and kindness towards her family and friends, adoring of her niece and the children of those who visited her in prison, yet had been responsible for the sadistic murder of other children. (Lee, 2010: 9)

This juxtaposition of Hindley as a kind person and Hindley as a murderer recalls Hannah Arendt's examination of evil. In *Eichmann in Jerusalem – A Report on the Banality of Evil* (2006), Arendt writes on the troubling (in)visibility of evil in regard to Adolf Eichmann, on trial for his part in the Nazi regime:

> The trouble with Eichmann was precisely that so many were like him, and that the many were neither perverted nor sadistic, that they were, and still are, terribly and terrifyingly normal. From the viewpoint of our legal institutions and of our moral standards of judgment, this normality was much more terrifying than all the atrocities put together. (Arendt, 2006: 276)

It is this false dichotomy between normal and evil that Marcus Harvey is interested in probing. Harvey explains that part of the reason Hindley was so widely condemned was for her lack of a 'normal' mothering instinct and the fact that she was a woman involved in the murder of children:

> This is the crucial issue: she didn't do the murdering, but she was a female who ignored her motherly instincts. That is her great crime. It was compounded by the unmentionable sin of looking like everybody's idea of what somebody who commits that crime should look like. (Burn, 2009: 395)

Thomson, too, seeks to investigate, and problematize, this binary throughout his novel. The reason why Hindley is so frightening is because she demonstrates that humans have the potential to carry out terrible crimes. The incomprehensible nature of Hindley's crime is a constant reminder of the depths to which humanity can sink:

That was what they meant, he realised, when they called her a monster. She had shown them what a human being was capable of. She had given them a glimpse of the horrific and terrifying acts that lay within their grasp. She had reminded them of a truth they had overlooked, or hidden from, or lied to themselves about. (*DM*, 198)

This raises the question of whether people who commit evil acts can ever be reformed. Billy realizes that it is the strength of public feeling that kept Hindley in jail, rather than an objective consideration of her position now. While other criminals, including murderers, are set free:

Clearly she was no danger to society. In fact, the opposite was true: were she to be released, society would be a danger to her. And here was the savage irony: taxpayers' money would have to be used to protect the woman from what the taxpayers themselves would try and do to her. (*DM*, 198)

As a result she was kept imprisoned by successive governments. The *idea* of Hindley – what she represented – rather than the real danger of her re-offending kept her imprisoned and so, it could be argued, the threat of evil was being policed. Here again is the idea that evil can be seen and controlled, with certain types of people identifiably malevolent.

Yet Thomson continually undercuts the idea that evil can be identified and demonstrates the impossibility of pinpointing truly malevolent people. The definition of evil is never fully worked out by Billy and questions are raised about whether certain areas, or people, have a higher propensity to commit criminal acts. Billy remembers when he put in a request to transfer to a new station to avoid more serious crimes:

One of the reasons why he'd put in for a transfer to Stowmarket at the beginning of the year was because it was such a sleepy little town, and the crime would be gentler, more trivial. That was the theory, anyway. (*DM*, 25)

However, as the novel progresses and various criminal or dangerous thoughts are expressed by Billy and Sue themselves, the existence of a stable, safe, normal life is shown to be an increasingly unsustainable idea: serious crimes can occur anywhere. Sue recounts a traumatic incident on a day trip to Whitby with Emma. On the cliffs, tired and strained from looking after a young disabled child, Sue imagines pushing Emma over the edge of the cliff, and how with her daughter's death all her problems would be solved (*DM*, 84). It is this potential for violence that Billy is so fascinated by, as he has seen it within himself. Sue's cold, selfish father is his first potential murder victim:

> He had realised that Newman was a man he could kill, and he would feel no qualms about it. He could use the onyx clock Sue's mother had given them when they got married [...] Battered to death with a present from his ex-wife. There was a nice symmetry to that. (*DM*, 45)

Billy here relishes the details of his potential crime and takes grim satisfaction from imagined violence. Murderous fantasies re-appear throughout the novel, with Billy threatening his ex-girlfriend Venetia's father, and Sue crashing her car and nearly killing their daughter Emma. The novel never settles the question of to what extent these murderous thoughts are part of being human.

Thomson had already explored the human potential for obsession, evil and violence in his earlier novel *The Book of Revelation* (1999). Here, the narrator is driven to attempted rape because of the abuse he has suffered at the hands of three mysterious women which raises the question of the effects of mental and physical abuse, and how violence can beget violence. Similarly in *Death of a Murderer* Billy discovers Venetia was abused by her father over a number of years and together they plot his death, yet their plans veer into the fantastical: 'What they were saying was so terrible that they got completely carried away, each attempting to outdo the other, their ideas becoming ever more lurid and unrealistic' (*DM*, 204). There is a sense that they have withdrawn from reality in order to cope with the horror of what has happened. This unreality recalls the narrator in *The Book of Revelation* who explains his lack of comprehension when facing his potential victim:

I stood in front of her, trying to remember. But there had been too many bodies. I was looking at this girl through the bodies of a hundred other girls. They were all still with me, inside my head, like interference. There was no clarity of signal, no clarity at all. (*BR*, 240)

The burden of the past weighs heavily on the narrator so that he can no longer see the present clearly. Like the possibilities of violence raised by the ghost of Hindley, the extent to which past events influence criminal acts is questioned and no conclusion is ever truly reached. Similarly, in *Divided Kingdom* (2005) Thomson describes a Britain of the future which has been divided into four distinct areas according to the medieval humours. The four areas have no contact with each other and families are divided in order that everyone can be put into their correct category. The areas are prohibited from mixing with each other. The narrator, Thomas Parry, is taken from his family as a child, and is placed with a foster family in the 'correct' area. As an adult, he becomes one of the workers who maintain and protect the status quo:

It was up to people like me, I thought, to safeguard the values and integrity of the Red Quarter. Only later did I start to understand why I might have been pushing myself so hard. I *had* to fight for the system, I *had* to believe in it, or my removal from my family would have all have been for nothing. (*DK*, 75)

What this highlights is Thomson's continuing interest in how structures of society encourage ways of thinking and the way that social structures encourage patterns of behaviour. Yet running alongside the social conditioning of individuals is the idea of the potential for evil within everyone, regardless of background. This juxtaposition is evident throughout *Death of a Murderer* where the murderous fantasies of Billy are evident beside his belief that the move to the quiet town of Stowmarket would produce crime that would be 'gentler, more trivial' (*DM*, 25). At odds throughout is the idea that certain crimes take place in certain places, caused by particular social circumstances, and the belief that crimes can be committed by anyone with potentially no warning sign.

(False) Memories of the past

Alongside calling into question the nature of evil, Hindley's ghost also interrogates the function of memory, and specifically how public and private memories become conflated. Hindley's ghost prompts Billy to remember his life in terms of public events. The omnipresence of the media has caused the prevalence of public events to be a symptom of modern life, with twenty-four hour rolling news and the ubiquity of the Internet increasingly dominating the way news is consumed. As Jameson (1991: 25) argues, history is produced with reference to our personal 'pop history' and 'we are condemned to seek history by way of our own pop images and simulacra of that history'. History, then, is increasingly linked to personal experiences and Billy remembers he would have been nine when the Moors Murders trial started (*DM*, 4). The lure of being part of history is reason enough to keep his guarding of Hindley's body a secret from his wife: 'They'd never kept too many secrets from each other – and besides, it was unusual, wasn't it? It was like being part of history' (*DM*, 6). This is a history that is tangible and that can be entered into. In part due to his childhood spent listening to stories of the Moors Murders, Billy has an interest in learning all he can about the crimes and re-visits the crime scenes. When visiting the Moors, Billy imagines that if he digs he might find 'a pair of spectacles, a shoe' (*DM*, 28) and uncover the paraphernalia of murdered children. Although the area has been dug up time and time again, he hopes to uncover the items which have not been recovered and to find a way to be further embedded within the (hi)story.

Part of the continuing popular fascination with Hindley, her crimes and her life in prison, is that she is from a time in Britain's history no longer recognizable at the beginning of the twenty-first century. Looking to her is a way of looking at the past. Hindley is a metonymic reminder of a time in Britain's past when society was changing with the post-war economic boom and an increase in social mobility:

> The combination of secular boom, full employment and a society of genuine mass consumption utterly transformed the lives of the working-class people in the developed countries, and continued to trans-

form it. By the standards of their parents, and indeed, if old enough, by their own memories, they were no longer poor. (Hobsbawm, 1994: 306)

People have never forgotten Hindley but they have increasingly forgotten the place she grew up in. The old Gorton area of Manchester that Hindley grew up in was lost by the 1980s, as Lee writes: 'It was swept away in the 1960s and 1970s, when town planners ordered its demolition as part of the city's slum-clearance programme [...] Ghosts of the old Gorton remain – the odd, mouldering pub and recognisable street name – but the rest has gone' (Lee, 2010: 29). Hindley is a reminder of the vanished worlds of the slums, and also of the tower blocks that replaced them – she is symbolic of a lost era of vanished utopianism. Avery F. Gordon develops Freud's argument that the ghost is an uncanny presence, not just of the person they once were but representative of the society they were part of, indeed:

> The ghost is not simply a dead or a missing person, but a social figure, and investigating it can lead to that dense site where history and subjectivity make social life. The ghost or the apparition is one form by which something lost, or barely visible, or seemingly not there to our supposedly well-trained eyes, makes itself known or apparent to us, in its own way of course. (Gordon, 2008: 8)

The melding of public and private memory continues throughout *Death of a Murderer*. Watching the Twin Towers fall on television Billy observes:

> They had no effect on him except as an illustration of his own private catastrophe. The demolished skyscrapers stood in for the car that Sue had reduced to a pile of scrap. The three thousand casualties symbolised her brush with death. It was his own story, written large. (*DM*, 121)

Whereas Hindley, for Billy, provides a continued emotional pull and fascination, the destruction of the Twin Towers only serves to remind him of his own personal circumstances. Hindley acts as a figure for Billy to interrogate his own past and he has attached special significance to her.

Furthermore, Hindley's ghost in the novel brings into question how events are remembered and the potential for false memories. Billy's chance encounter with his childhood friend Trevor takes a dark turn when Trevor reveals he was picked up by Hindley and, after being taken to an anonymous room, managed to make a lucky escape from almost certain death: 'I'm linked to them for ever, those children. The ones with the names we all know. Sometimes it's like I can sense their presence – somewhere near by' (*DM*, 140). Trevor ultimately commits suicide, as Billy is led to believe, due to the horror of this encounter and subsequent survivor's guilt:

> Not only had Trevor survived, but he had also kept the fact of his survival to himself. If he had told his parents what had happened – the woman in the white car, the man on the motorbike – if he had identified the house, it was possible that lives could have been saved. (*DM*, 140)

Yet after thinking about the turn of events, Billy wonders if such a thing can be possible – he can find no mention of Trevor, or escaped children, in any of the official accounts. This makes him wonder whether the fact that Trevor was about to lose his job, coupled with the pressure of having to support his large family, might have allowed him to create false memories in order to blame his current predicament on past events: 'In the excitement of that chance encounter, he had overlooked the most important factors: Trevor had a large family – four children – and was about to lose his job. He would have been under enormous strain' (*DM*, 151). It is this strain that may have distorted Trevor's thinking and caused him to either fictionalize or misremember events. The murders committed by Hindley and Brady are so embedded in the national psyche that the line between participant and observer has become blurred: 'No one who had been alive at the time could ever be entirely free of it. It was one of those rare news items against which you defined yourself' (*DM*, 155). This demonstrates the extent to which these crimes have influenced other lives and again suggests that it is in the nature of certain crimes to grab the public imagination. Doubting Trevor's childhood experience also raises questions about the validity of Billy witnessing the ghost of

Hindley in the hospital car park, and not just witnessing the ghost, but interacting with her. Like Trevor, Billy is under enormous pressure in his home life where he faces an unhappy marriage, extra-marital affairs, miscarriages and a daughter with Down's Syndrome – home is a place he avoids. Billy has also demonstrated an (over) interest in the Moors Murders, researching the case and re-visiting the Moors. Like Trevor's memories, it might be reasonable to assume that the ghost of Hindley is merely the expression of an over-wrought imagination. Yet the unremarkable nature of Hindley's ghost, appearing in a catalogue suit rather than sporting the blonde beehive of popular imagination, signals that the ghost is actually 'real', that is, Hindley's ghost is a manifestation of Hindley's life experiences and not just a vision of her most iconic image. This again emphasizes Thomson's interest in Hindley's life as a whole and the after-life of her imprisonment. By rendering the ghost a mundane version of Hindley, Billy is able to listen to her and not immediately dismiss her as the creation of his over-wrought imagination. The ghost does not appear to scare Billy, but rather to prompt him to consider his own life: her function is, ironically, to make him realize what he has achieved in his life and to problematize the human capacity for evil. As Gordon argues:

> Being haunted draws us affectively, sometimes against our will and always a bit magically, into the structure of feeling of a reality we come to experience, not as cold knowledge, but as a transformative recognition. (Gordon, 2008: 8)

Billy's confrontation of past events throughout the novel is a transformative experience for him. At the end of the novel, while bathing Emma, his mind races to the future: 'Would she always live at home, with them? Who would care for her when they were dead?' (*DM*, 249). Yet instead of dwelling on these future worries, he is able to see clearly, perhaps for the first time, his daughter for what she is in the present: 'Looking at his daughter stretched out in the bath, he noticed how strong her body was, and how well made, her skin so sleek and rosy, so unblemished' (*DM*, 249). Here, at the very end, there is a sense that Billy has achieved a sense of peace and he is no longer haunted by past events. Whereas the ghost of Hindley draws Billy into his past, in contrast, Emma forces him to engage in his present. There is nothing uncanny about her and so in her presence Billy is free from his ghosts.

In *Death of a Murderer* the appearance of Hindley's ghost to policeman Billy Tyler prompts him to consider his life to date. Hindley's ghost is an uncanny presence in a novel which is filled with uncanny moments and her corporeal and unremarkable form make her crimes even more frightening. Aside from her iconic mug-shot, Thomson's Hindley is jarringly mundane and not the totem of evil that she is so frequently called upon to symbolize. To Billy, Hindley is a ghost that has haunted his past and continues to haunt his present as he is unable to extricate his life from her crimes. In re-thinking his past Billy considers how close he has come to committing evil acts himself and demonstrates how Hindley is not so far removed from him, she is not the distant criminal of the popular imagination. The most frightening element of Thomson's novel is his problematizing of the concepts of good and evil and highlighting the potential of evil that exists within everyone. Evil cannot be easily identified or read upon people's faces and there is a tension between social structures which seek to control evil and the knowledge that malevolent acts can happen anywhere and be committed by anyone. Furthermore, Thomson explores, through the ghost of Hindley, the potential for creating collective false memories – like the morality in the novel, memory is problematic. Hindley is a metonym for a darker version of the 1960s but she also figures as a cornerstone in (false) personal memories. The ever presence of news means that history is consumed with reference to our own personal narratives, so much so that the line between the personal and the public can become blurred as demonstrated by Billy and Trevor's memories. *Death of a Murderer* is a complex novel where life, death, fact, fiction, public and private are all uncomfortably interwoven and absolute certainties are unattainable.

Works Cited

Arendt, Hannah (2006) *Eichmann in Jerusalem: A Report on the Banality of Evil*. London: Penguin Classics.

BBC News (2008) '2012 Hindley image use condemned', 25 August, URL (consulted December 2014), http://news.bbc.co.uk/1/hi/uk/7580261. stm

BBC News (2012) 'Ian Brady "may have revealed Keith Bennett burial place"', 17 August, URL (consulted April 2015): http://www.bbc.co.uk/news/uk-england-19292164

Burn, Gordon (1991) *Alma Cogan*. London: Minerva.

Burn, Gordon (2009) *Sex & Violence, Death & Silence: Encounters with Recent Art*. London: Faber and Faber.

Derrida, Jacques (1994) *Spectres of Marx*, trans. Peggy Kamuf. London: Routledge.

Fisher, Mark (2014) *Ghosts of My Life: Writings on Depression, Hauntology and Lost Futures*. Winchester: Zero Books.

Freud, Sigmund (2003) *The Uncanny, trans. David McLintock*. London: Penguin Classics.

Gordon, Avery F. (2008) *Ghostly Matters*. Minneapolis: University of Minnesota Press.

Haggard, H. Rider (2008) *She*. Oxford: Oxford University Press.

Hobsbawn, Eric (1994) *The Age of Extremes 1914–1991*. London: Abacus.

Hutcheon, Linda (1989) *The Politics of Postmodernism*. London: Routledge.

Jameson, Fredric (1991) *Postmodernism, Or The Cultural Logic of Late Capitalism*. London: Verso.

Lee, Carol Ann (2010) *One of Your Own: The Life and Death of Myra Hindley*. Edinburgh: Mainstream Publishing.

Sapsted, David and Nigel Bunyan (2002) 'Myra Hindley, the Moors monster, dies after 36 years in jail', *Telegraph*, 16 November, URL (consulted April 2014): http://www.telegraph.co.uk/news/uknews/1413341/Myra-Hindley-the-Moors-monster-dies-after-36-years-in-jail.html

Shaw, Katy (2011) *David Peace: Texts and Contexts*. Eastbourne: Sussex Academic Press.

Sun (2002) 'Evil Myra Hindley Dead', URL (consulted April 2014): http://www.thesun.co.uk/sol/homepage/news/152691/Evil-Myra-Hindley-dead.html

'THE SHAME OF BEING A MAN'
SHAME, MASCULINITY AND WRITING IN *THE BOOK OF REVELATION*

Kaye Mitchell

'The shame of being a man – is there any better reason to write?', asks Gilles Deleuze, in an essay entitled simply 'Literature and Life' (Deleuze, 1997: 225). (It occurs to me, incidentally, that the shame of being a *woman* might too often be adduced as a reason *not* to write). Notably, Deleuze's statement sits alongside his assertion that, in writing, 'one becomes-woman, becomes-animal or -vegetable, becomes-molecule, to the point of becoming-imperceptible' (Deleuze, 1997: 225). In other words, this is part of an argument about the (necessary) disintegration of authority and dominance – even of identity itself – in the act of writing, where 'man' equals 'a dominant form of expression that claims to impose itself on all matter, whereas woman, animal, or molecule always has a component of flight that escapes its own formalization.' (Deleuze, 1997: 225) Writing, then, facilitates an escape from the shame of 'being a man' in this quite specific sense.

Steven Connor, in a 2000 paper (later published as a shorter article) on the 'shame of being a man', offers a subtle contestation of Deleuze's point for his own ends, commenting that:

> To write is not to free oneself from the shame of being a man, or not, at least, but for sure, if you are this one. Writing might also be a way

of meeting with shame, a coming in to male shamefulness. I have sur-
prised myself by wanting to be able to conclude that male shame, or
my kind, is less to be regretted than one might at first think. (Connor,
2000: n.p.)

In doing so, he sets up a discussion of the triangular relation between
shame, masculinity and writing, while also positing shame as an affect
that is both inextricable from maleness and at least partly desirable:
inextricable, thanks to a growing awareness (presumably as a result of
feminism) of 'the shamefulness of being a man as such and at all', and
hence desirable in the move towards more enlightened gender roles,
but also ever-present in the anxiety around 'falling short of being a
man' (Connor, 2000: n.p.). Both successful and unsuccessful performances of masculinity – whatever the criteria of 'success' might be
– therefore have the potential to induce shame. Wayne Koestenbaum
(2011: 7), who is less concerned with the role that writing might play
in 'meeting with' male shame (though he does suggest that humiliation 'is the feared and inevitable outcome of most writing, especially
if it knows itself to be writing'), nevertheless comes to similar conclu-
sions in his recent book on humiliation,[1] averring that:

> 'Masculinity,' however questionable a property, and however much
> women also possess it, is something that can be seen as humiliating
> (it is humiliating to have a penis, it is humiliating not to have a womb)
> or as something that can be *taken away* by humiliation (a man who is
> humiliated has less of a penis than he did before the humiliation oc-
> curred). (Koestenbaum, 2011: 10)

Koestenbaum's subsequent, numerous, personal examples of frustrated or repudiated desire go some way towards explaining why it might
be 'humiliating to have a penis', mitigating the apparent glibness of
this claim: its offhand dismissal of female masculinity; its too-facile
appropriation of a lack traditionally conceived as feminine. Yet for
Koestenbaum too, humiliation is no bad thing, indeed the experience
of it may constitute 'a passport to decency and civilization, [...] a
necessary shedding of hubris' (Koestenbaum, 2011: 3), particularly,
he implies, as far as men are concerned.

In this chapter, I take Connor's and Koestenbaum's thoughts as starting points for thinking through the complex relations between shame, gender and writing, in order to show precisely the difficulty of acknowledging or of owning shame, for a man, but also the obstacles to writing masculine shame. Too often, I suggest, writing is used not as a way of 'coming in to male shamefulness', but rather to displace or disavow shame in order to shore up precisely the model of masculinity that Connor, for example, eschews as shameful; such attempts at mastery-through-writing are either profoundly un-Deleuzian, or, in the light of Deleuze's comments, particularly futile. Martin Amis's *The Pregnant Widow* (2010), which I will consider in due course, is one such instance of a novel that seeks to displace male shamefulness (particularly sexual shame) onto vulnerable female bodies; by contrast, Rupert Thomson's 1999 novel, *The Book of Revelation*, offers us a way in to thinking about the more complex and challenging politics and poetics of male shamefulness. The protagonist's ordeal in *The Book of Revelation* is an exercise in the ambivalent effects and affects of shame; his response to that ordeal, following his release, rehearses a dismantling of identity which is more than simply a stock response to trauma; instead it posits the limitations of masculine identity, conventionally understood, in the negotiation of experiences of abasement and victimhood. Whether the acts of narration and writing counteract or compound that dismantling of (authorial, authoritative, masculine) identity, is a question I will also consider here.

Shame and gender

If shame is 'an inner torment, a sickness of the soul', in the words of Silvan Tomkins, it is also an emotion of self-assessment, a peculiarly *social* experience and, I would suggest, a culturally pervasive affect with particular pertinence for understanding contemporary constructions of gendered subjectivity, expressions and experiences of sexual desire, the complexities of embodiment, and social processes of 'othering' (Tomkins, 1995: 133). Its relationship to processes of subjectivation is a singularly complex one: as Gershen Kaufman tells us, 'no other affect is more disturbing to the self, none more central for the sense of identity', in the way that it works, simultaneously, to shore up and to threaten a sense of self in relation to, and in contradistinction from, others (Kaufman, 1989: viii). Writing in 2007, Ruth Leys claimed that, 'Today, shame (and shamelessness) has displaced guilt as a dominant emotional reference in the West', arguing that there has been 'a major paradigm shift', a 'broad shift [...] in the medical and psychiatric sciences, literary criticism, and even philosophy away from the "moral" concept of guilt in favor of the ethically different or "freer" concept of shame' (Leys, 2007: 4, 7). The recent critical interest in shame has emerged in and across various fields and disciplines: in psychoanalysis (Nathanson, 1988, 1992); in philosophical work which, contra Leys, does still tend to regard shame as a 'moral' emotion (Nussbaum, 2004; Taylor, 1985; Williams, 1993); as part of Holocaust studies (Agamben, 2008; Levi, 1979, 1988; Leys, 2007; Morgan, 2008); within feminism (Bartky, 1990; Lehtinen, 1998; Manion, 2003); and, most recently, within queer theory, as part of a wider interest in negative affect which seeks to complicate the pride discourse of earlier decades (Halperin and Traub, 2009; Love, 2007; Munt, 2007; Probyn, 2005; Sedgwick, 1993, 2003). Significantly, much of the recent theorizing has offered 'a reevaluation that casts shame as at least potentially a positive, not a destructive emotion', and, notes Leys (2007: 124), 'for some theorists, indeed, shame serves at the limit as a site of resistance to cultural norms of identity.'

As Leys (2007: 11) also observes, 'by common agreement, guilt concerns your actions' – actual or fantasized – while shame 'is held to concern not your actions but who you are, that is, your deficiencies and inadequacies as a person as these are revealed to the shaming gaze of the other'. It is particularly telling, then, that historically, shame has been associated primarily with femininity – indeed the classical personification of shame (and humility, reverence, etc.) is a woman: Aidos.[2] In her 1990 book, *Femininity and Domination*, Sandra Bartky explores the relationship between gender and shame, suggesting that shame is one of those 'patterns of mood and feeling' that tends 'to characterize women more than men' (Bartky, 1990: 84). As she explains:

To say that some pattern of feeling in women, say shame, is gender-related is not to claim that it is gender-specific, i.e. that men are never ashamed; it is only to claim that women are more prone to experience the emotion in question and that the feeling itself has a different meaning in relation to their total psychic situation and general social location than has a similar emotion when experienced by men. (Bartky, 1990: 84)

Men may feel shame at failing to attain levels of power, influence or success expected of them *as men*, while for women shame may be a kind of generalized condition of being a woman in the world. So shame traditionally signals a loss, lack or failure of masculinity on the part of men, but is part of the condition of – indeed, is constitutive of – femininity; male and female shame, then, as Bartky explains here, have different meanings (and effects) psychically and socially. The shame that Bartky (1990: 85) characterizes as feminine is manifested as 'a pervasive sense of personal inadequacy' and 'a pervasive affective attunement to the social environment'. Subsequent critics have echoed Bartky's claim that 'the female socialization process can be viewed as a prolonged immersion in shame' (Bouson, 2009: 2), though the gendering of shame (as feminine) actually receives relatively little attention in philosophical, psychoanalytic and queer accounts of it.

Koestenbaum echoes the idea of shame as a *loss* or failure of masculinity, thus witnessing a humiliated man, 'fills [him] with horror'; but he also feels that the 'maleness' of the humiliated man 'has received a necessary puncture' (Koestenbaum, 2011: 23). Yet if Koestenbaum's reflections on humiliation seem to offer a more radical take on the relation of shame and humiliation to gender, they still betray a grounding in a more conventional account. Humiliation, on his (avowedly subjective and idiosyncratic) reading equals a 'collapse' of maleness, but not of femaleness – indeed, arguably it is a confirmation of femaleness; Koestenbaum (2011: 10) notes that, 'from some points of view, womanliness or femininity is a humiliated quality'. Our understanding of humiliation and shame, then, both proceeds from and confirms, even perpetuates, a binaristic understanding of gender. In fact, if we view shame as functioning, in Freudian terms, as a kind of 'watchman' or 'guardian', what it polices is not 'morality' (the Freudian view) so much as patriarchal gender norms.[3]

If men and women stand in different relations to shame, then it is perhaps predictable that they might write it differently. So, although there is, as Connor (2000: n.p.) notes, 'a strong male tradition of attempting to write the weakness of shame' – he mentions Melville, Kafka, Beckett, Genet, Coetzee – women writers have generally sought to '[write] themselves out of shame rather than into it'. It is that 'redemptive' aspect of women's writing on/of shame that is picked up, for example, by J. Brooks Bouson (2009: 15) in her readings of Toni Morrison and others, whom she portrays as seeking a 'remedy to shame', and as 'providing a very powerful critique of the cultural narratives that shame women'. This tendency to see literary engagements with shame as broadly critical and redemptive, part of a process of *overcoming* or conquering shame, is a common one;[4] meanwhile, when women authors engage with supposedly shameful topics in more ambivalent, less redemptive ways, they are apt to receive censure for doing so.[5] Does this then make it easier for male authors to 'meet with' shame – or does it only give them licence to write about 'shameful' topics? Is an admission of shame even possible without a compromising – rather than, more positively, a transformation – of conventional masculinity? Must it involve a transmutation of shame into guilt (what Connor terms 'the desire to get shame to run along guilt's grooves'), or into masochism (and thus into another kind of dominance, through willed subjection) (Connor, 2000: n.p.)? As Connor (2000: n.p.) asserts, 'male shame [...] has a crudely and traditionally heroic aspect [...]. It is hard for men to write in shame without attempting to coin glory from it'. *The Book of Revelation*, I will proceed to argue, attempts an encounter with shame that resists masculine heroism at each turn – in its narration as well as the developments that make up its plot.

Masculinity and shame in contemporary fiction

At first glance, recent novels by established, canonical authors such as Ian McEwan, Martin Amis and Philip Roth evince a notable concern with masculine shame, with sexual embarrassment and disappointment, impotence, and the ageing male body – consider, for example, *On Chesil Beach* (2007), *Exit Ghost* (2007), *The Humbling* (2009), and *The Pregnant Widow* (2010). However, these apparent interventions into the sphere of masculine shame too often bear out Connor's central point that, from the standpoint of masculinity, shame too easily becomes a form of heroism, a badge of pride. Additionally, the *apparent* confession of shame is, in these novels, too often mitigated by the ultimate displacement of that shame upon female bodies. On the differences between male and female shame, Connor (2000: n.p.) writes that, 'Women are shamed for breaking out, men are ashamed of falling short. Female shame has mostly been regulatory and disciplinary'; and texts like *The Pregnant Widow* confirm Connor's claim.

The Pregnant Widow opens with the assertion that: 'This is the story of a sexual trauma', which 'ruined him for twenty-five years' (Amis, 2010: 1). What is the nature of this ruination, this trauma? Certainly it involves a kind of sexual shame or, more precisely, a bewilderment, on the part of protagonist Keith Nearing, in the face of the changing rules of sexual engagement. On Amis's reading, these changes spell shame for both men and women: men are 'shamed' by feminism (they bear their masculinity, consequently, *as shame*); but women suffer the greater shame for violating the codes of femininity. For it is ruined female bodies – notably those of the protagonist's promiscuous, alcoholic sister, Violet, and his sexually voracious lover, Gloria – which bear the shame of the unstable, shifting mores of the sexual revolution. Violet, notable mainly for her 'extreme sexual delinquency' (she is 'the kind of girl who dates football teams') and her alcoholism, dies of a heart attack at the age of 46 (Amis, 2010: 298, 299). In interviews around the book's publication, Amis reiterated the suggestion that the 'chaos' and 'desolation'[6] of the sexual and feminist revolutions (he fails to distinguish between the two) had been visited upon women's bodies, in his acknowledgement that Violet is modelled on his sister Sally Amis, who he described as 'pathologically promiscuous' and 'one of the most spectacular victims of the revolution' (Flood, 2009). Sally, he claimed, 'was just harming herself', as were other women caught up in the 'equalitarian phase' of feminism in 'going against their natures' by 'behaving like [boys]' (Lawson, 2010). Whether this behaviour invites shame/shaming or merely confirms the already latent and inescapable shame of femininity is, in *The Pregnant Widow*, hard to decipher.

Visiting Violet in 'the Church Army Hostel for Young Women', Keith asks Gloria, 'Why are the girls so silent?', and she replies, 'Because they've been shamed beyond words' (Amis, 2010: 437–8). Indeed, Violet loses any ability or right to speak for herself, becoming simply a ruined body (the ruin both a sign of her shame and a peculiarly literal punishment for it), to be 'levered' out from under some unsuitable man each morning (Amis, 2010: 405). Her speech is debased, disintegrating, just as her body is: 'It really is remarkable: to attempt so little in the way of language – and to bugger *that* up', thinks Keith, 'Wiv, fanks, elfy: the explanation for all this would belatedly occur to him' (Amis, 2010: 433). In his extra-textual musings about Sally/Violet, Amis comments that, 'you would have needed the Taliban to control her. If she'd been conditioned by a really strong culture of self-denial, she might have made it, although in any kind of shame-and-honour arrangement she would already have been killed by her father, her uncle and brother' (Long, 2010). Amis, despite his anti-Islamic sentiments within and beyond the novel, actually sets great store by a 'shame-and-honour' culture (Is this what feminism has done away with, in his view?) and *The Pregnant Widow* arguably enacts a secular version of such a culture in its treatment of its female characters.

In *The Pregnant Widow*, then, female shame is disciplinary and systemic. Acknowledging the distinction between the kind of shame that 'is a tonic episode in the life of a subject' and the 'systemic sense of undervaluation' considered by Frantz Fanon (in *Black Skin, White Masks*) and Sandra Bartky (in *Femininity and Domination*), Connor (2000: n.p.) concedes that 'the kind of shame which allows one room to reserve judgement on oneself is not really shame at all'. For Keith, such shame as *he* experiences can be no more than 'a tonic episode', while the shame of Violet and Gloria, respectively, pertains to a 'systemic sense of undervaluation'; fundamentally, Amis refuses to challenge that system or question that undervaluation; he cannot, or will not, face up to the shame of being a man.

These examples imply an awareness of what Lynne Segal has described as the 'masculinity in crisis' literature (in sociology, gender studies, etc.) of the 1990s, but they can also be read as part of the 'backlash' against feminism that views the feminist attempt to 'reform masculinity' *as* a crisis, rather than a positive development (Segal, 2001: 237). To this, Segal responds:

> The 'masculinity in crisis' literature is problematic insofar as it ignores the central issue: the pay-offs men receive (or hope to receive) from their claims to manhood. For while men everywhere express their anxieties and loss of former privileges, overall they are conceived of and remain the dominant sex. (Segal, 2001: 239)

The 'source' of the crisis is not feminism, but the fact that masculinity 'condenses a certain engagement with power' that is 'largely unrealizable', and thus 'masculinity is always in crisis' (Segal, 2001: 239). Daniel Lea and Berthold Schoene, in their introduction to *Posting the Male*, suggest that masculinity has, in the contemporary period, 'become visible as a performative gender construct, and a rather frail and fraudulent one to boot', but they 'prefer to speak of masculinity as a gender "in transition" rather than a gender "in crisis"' (Lea and Schoene, 2003: 9, 11). Are more nuanced and suggestive literary engagements with masculinity and shame than Amis's to be found – with a masculinity 'in transition' (or even, more precisely, with *the shame of being a man*)? I will turn now to *The Book of Revelation*.

The Book of Revelation

In this disconcerting, elusive novel, the protagonist (a young male ballet dancer who is never named) is kidnapped by a trio of cloaked, hooded women and held captive for eighteen days, during which period he is chained up, sexually violated, verbally and physically abused, forced to perform for his captors, and physically mutilated. The difficulty of articulating masculine shame is evidenced by the novel's central formal conceit: a switch from first to third person at the moment of kidnap, and a switch back at the moment of release, so that for eighteen days he surrenders the power of the speaking 'I' and becomes simply 'he', 'the man'; during this period he is defined by his objectification and his lack of agency. Those eighteen days are cut off from the rest of his life, forming a surreal interlude, a break in his everyday reality which then throws that 'reality' into turmoil and doubt; in fact he is unable to return to the life that he had prior to the kidnapping, subsequently forsaking both his career and his relationship with his girlfriend. Meanwhile, the bare and unmodulated manner of the narration throughout has a deflationary effect upon what might otherwise be melodramatic or titillating material.

In temporarily denying his protagonist a (first-person) voice with which to describe the immediate experience of shameful and shaming abuse, Thomson's text invokes the question of the extent to which shame can be spoken (or written). As Connor avers, 'properly, innocently shamed people have no words at their disposal, with which to clear their muddied names. Shame is bottomless, there is far too much ever to tell of it, and so it holds its tongue.' (Connor, 2000: n.p.) For Timothy Bewes, shame is similarly unspeakable: 'shame resists interpretation, since to speak of it boldly, adequately, is to counteract it, to produce its opposite – or itself as its own opposite (shame as absence of shame)' (Bewes, 2011: 3). And, in the work of certain writers (Bewes considers Kafka and Coetzee, among others), 'shame seems to be a placeholder for a quality or a modality of thought that cannot adequately be accounted for by language, or reduced to what is expressible in language' (Bewes, 2011: 14).[7] Indeed, for Bewes, shame is, more profoundly, the 'material embodiment' of a 'tension between the ethical and aesthetic dimensions of literature', which points up, 'a moment at which the formal possibilities open to the work are incommensurable with, or simply inadequate to, its ethical responsibilities' (Bewes, 2011: 1). So shame is always a matter of form as well as content – something that most critical writing on shame and literature fails to recognize – and it reveals the limitations of writing, the shame attached to writing itself (as a duplicitous, fatally compromised, inadequate exercise), and the sense (in the period of modernity) that language is 'constitutively untrustworthy' (Bewes, 2011: 12), thanks to its indeterminate origins, semantic instability and uncertain effects. The switch from first to third person in Thomson's novel, then, explicitly refuses various kinds of mastery (authorial, aesthetic, formal, masculine) in relation to shame and, by extension, resists the logic of overcoming found in other literary engagements with shame, as well as the critical responses to them. This apparent refusal of mastery is itself an example of authorial mastery – a double-bind that, presumably, no text can escape – yet the temporary cessation of the first-person voice effects a deliberate undermining of the protagonist's authority, renders his interiority a little more opaque, makes his subjectivity (so often achieved, in novels, via the medium of voice) a little more uncertain, and withholds the consolations of cathartic expression.

Furthermore, in *The Book of Revelation* the complexities of the man's initial response to his capture and violation are striking. We are told: 'He felt nothing but shame and humiliation. No, wait. That wasn't entirely true. There had been another feeling there, a feeling that lurked behind the others, shadowy and sly – insidious: a feeling of excitement' (*BR*, 25). Koestenbaum claims that, 'An iota of sexual excitement – reparative, compensatory – surrounds the subject of humiliation' (Koestenbaum, 2011: 24), but if this seems like mere prurience then he goes further in his repeated linking of humiliation and pleasure, whether this is a pleasure in the humiliation of others, in the witnessing of humiliation, or a pleasure in being humiliated. Either way, pleasure is never far away in Koestenbaum's account of humiliation (including 'the pleasure of being a spectacle', and the finding of 'a new community, a fellowship – across history – of sufferers and outcasts', something that the protagonist of *The Book of Revelation* notably fails to do) (Koestenbaum, 2011: 8, 9). In Thomson's novel, the protagonist's feeling of excitement produces, in turn, a further sense of shame for it betrays what Tomkins calls 'interest'; for Tomkins, shame, like disgust, 'operates ordinarily only after interest or enjoyment has been activated, and inhibits one or the other or both. The innate activator of shame is the incomplete reduction of interest or joy.' (Tomkins, 1995: 134) So, as the man struggles with feelings of complicity, his shame is not unmixed with desire (an 'interest' on the part of his body that his mind repudiates):

> What sort of man is it, he thought, who just submits? [...] Had the women identified some kind of need in him? Had he tacitly encouraged them? Was he, in some fundamental sense, responsible for all this? (BR, 26)

What makes this shameful – rather than merely distressing or embarrassing – is both his perceived complicity in what is taking place and the failure of masculinity that is (in his distorted view of things) both cause and effect of his ordeal. This goes beyond the self-denigrating *guilt* of the victim to encompass a more fundamental *shame*, illuminating the point that, while guilt relates to something you have *done*, shame announces a flaw in what or who you *are*. Ultimately he begins to feel:

> As if his fate was no more or less than he deserved. There was nothing random or accidental about what had happened to him. There was nothing *unlucky* about it. All those years of performing on stage – exhibiting himself... What was dance if it was not exposure of the body? It was as though he had advertised himself. (BR, 92–3)

At first glance, the 'fault' that the protagonist identifies appears to be a fairly conventional one of a failure of masculinity: 'what sort of man is it [...] who just submits?' Even this 'exhibition' of himself is implicitly feminized (because it is femininity that invites the gaze, and the status of object, in this way) so, he thinks, he was already at fault, even before the kidnapping. Once in the control of the three women, he is reduced to the position of feminine objectification – indeed, when one of the women rapes him, using a dildo, she says to him, 'You know what you are, don't you, [...] You're a cunt', and repeats the word 'cunt' as she rapes him (BR, 46). This would seem to suggest that the shame he experiences is the shame of being, symbolically at least, a woman; more than this, in becoming a 'cunt', he becomes something to be penetrated, violated, a space, a lack.

As Koestenbaum (2011: 8) explains, 'Humiliation, a topsy-turvy regime, involves a reversal: from top to bottom, from high to low, from exalted to degraded, from secure to insecure.' Given the gendered nature of humiliation, this implies a move from exalted masculinity to 'degraded' effeminacy in the experience of male shame. Yet the shame explored in *The Book of Revelation* goes beyond a shame at failed masculinity and unwanted effeminacy: in the novel's suggestion of the protagonist's own complicity/arousal, but also in its invocation of childhood and of a more profound desubjectification. There is something distinctly maternal in the women's care for the protagonist (a factor that sits oddly with their frequent cruelty), in the way that they wash and dry him, feed and tend him; yet even that apparent 'care' is shaming, signalling, on his part, a kind of bodily dependency, a return to the childhood scene of shame,[8] the child's dependence on the mother (and again this is a kind of disgust aimed at himself, rather than projected outwards). When one of the women takes him to the toilet, he thinks: 'it felt odd to be handled that way. It had brought back a period of his life that he had thought was lost for ever. With just a few simple actions, she had closed a gap of thirty years, returning him to his first few moments in the world' (*BR*, 21). Throughout, the experience of imprisonment and abuse is both eroticized and infantilizing – the 'ten-foot chain running from his pierced foreskin to the iron staple in the wall' seeming to the man 'like a surreal version of an umbilical cord', but one which yet signals his peculiarly sexual subjection – and it is this conjunction of the erotic and the infantile (amongst other things) that produces his feeling of shame (*BR*, 85).

As his ordeal continues, the man's very identity is under threat; it is this fragmentation of identity, this undoing of self (again, beyond merely an unseating of masculinity) that is the real subject of the book, and shame plays a crucial role in that undoing. The suggestion that shame is both constitutive and disruptive of subjectivity features frequently in its theorization – indeed, Giorgio Agamben defines shame as:

Nothing less than the fundamental sentiment of being *a subject*, in the two apparently opposed senses of this phrase: to be subjected and to be sovereign. Shame is what is produced in the absolute concomitance of subjectification and desubjectification, self-loss and self-possession, servitude and sovereignty. (Agamben, 2008: 107)

In its painstakingly impersonal narration of the man's experience of imprisonment and abuse (his loss of a voice, his changing relationship with his body, his acute self-consciousness and moments of self-blaming which are yet coincident with a vertiginous loss of purposive selfhood), Thomson's novel explores this 'absolute concomitance of subjectification and desubjectification'. In the 'desubjectification' of humiliation, claims Koestenbaum (2011: 29), 'the subject ceases to be a subject and becomes a thing acted upon', but here that experience of desubjectification is complicated and refined via a subtle understanding of the gendered and erotic dimensions of the shame experience.

Thus, while the protagonist is still a captive, we are told:

Sometimes he would catch a glimpse of himself in one of the steel rings that held his wrists. He could only ever see himself in fragments. A cheekbone, an eyebrow. Part of an ear. He was like a vase that had been broken thousands of years ago. He would never be whole again. He only existed in pieces. In memory. (BR, 78)

This inability to see himself whole continues throughout the narrative. While the use of the incomplete mirror image is a quite familiar way of signalling identity breakdown (albeit complicated by his mirror being one of the steel rings that imprisons him, a neat touch), the simile of the shattered vase is an interestingly aestheticized and gendered one – invoking quite feminine connotations of beauty, fragility, value, artistry and vulnerability. In this shattering of his identity he becomes infant, woman, precious vase, but also animal: as the women undress him we are told that 'his clothes [are] laid open, peeled back, like the skin of an animal that was being dissected' (BR, 23). And later, following his mutilation, he thinks: 'That low groaning he could hear, a sound that was so constant, so present in the room that it seemed to have a form – a dog run over by a car, a coat thrown on the ground – that groaning sound, that was him' (BR, 78–9). These are images of powerlessness; the whole ordeal itself is 'like a lesson in which he had been taught the true meaning of the word "powerlessness"', a shaming that does more than emasculate him, it dehumanizes him (*BR*, 47).

In addition to exploring the unsettling and erotic force of powerlessness, *The Book of Revelation* evinces an awareness of the power of shame as spectacle – that is, its visual power and the extent to which it is experienced as an excessive or tormenting but also exhilarating *visibility*, to oneself and to others; again, as Tomkins tells us, 'In shame I wish to continue to look and to be looked at, but I also do not wish to do so' (Tomkins, 1995: 137); this is the peculiar ambivalence of the shame response. Sartre famously described shame as 'the recognition of the fact that I am indeed that object which the Other is looking at and judging' (Sartre, 1958: 210). So in the man's encounters with the three women their gaze is eroticized; their power lies in the fact that they can see him – and they spend a great deal of time looking at him, watching him – but he cannot see them behind their hoods or masks. Their own shame, if they feel any, is not therefore visible (though the most reluctant of his kidnappers, who he names Maude, might be said to carry shame in her very bearing and physicality, with her 'red, slightly swollen knuckles' and 'bitten fingernails' [*BR*, 15], her 'heavy and dimpled thighs', 'ample belly' and 'solid, rounded shoulders' [*BR*, 70], somehow expressing her 'downtrodden, almost masochistic nature' [*BR*, 50]). The room, with its emptiness, bare white walls and single skylight, is perfectly set up for the 'performances' (sexual and artistic) that the women force him to enact; it is 'an artificial space, a setting – a kind of stage', he realizes, and the ritualistic nature of the women's actions confirms their awareness of what they are doing as spectacle, even when no other audience is present (*BR*, 48).

Following his release, the man finds that he is (serially) unable to 'unburden' himself, even when much depends on it. It is not only that his shame stops him speaking (as if it were his own fault he would be confessing and as if to do so would further undermine his beleaguered masculinity); more fundamentally, he lacks basic recognition, acknowledgement. At home, alone, immediately after his release, he sits with the French windows open and the air on his skin makes him feel 'as if I had been acknowledged at long last. I could tell where I began and ended, how much space I occupied. I knew the limits of my-self, and it was something, to know that.' (*BR*, 119) This 'recognition' is what makes him a subject in the eyes of others – he needs it yet also fears exposure to that coruscating, constituting/subjectivating gaze; he retreats to a solitary spot in the countryside because, 'I didn't want to be seen, by anyone' – a notably passive construction (*BR*, 134); as before his shame has made him painfully visible. His travels (or, more accurately, wanderings) over the course of the next three years are not a search for self ('I wasn't looking for anything, least of all myself') (*BR*, 156), but they form part of a longer-term transformation:

> Every now and then I remembered how I had stood outside that bar on the day of my release, and how *I had failed to recognise myself*. I now thought of that as a defining moment. During my time in the white room, I had started to undergo some sort of transformation. My blond hair, my brown skin – they were just superficial changes. More significant by far was the fact that my relationship with my body had altered and altered radically. [...] My body was no longer the centre of my attention, no longer the instrument through which I expressed myself, and, as a result, my life had lost much of its focus. (*BR*, 158; emphasis added)

The nature of this 'transformation' is never fully expounded, but cer-tainly in his new life the man seems to take refuge in an unemotional lifestyle of secrecy, excessive promiscuity, displacement and aggres-sion, displaying ultimately a kind of parodic/hegemonic masculin-ity in which he is ill at ease; the sex without 'personal involvement' that he pursues as a way of hunting down the women who kidnapped him does 'not come naturally' to him and he fears he is 'beginning to resemble' the many men for whom that behaviour is 'natural' (*BR*, 184). Yet this is not simply a kind of masculine acting-out to rid him-self of the shame of his apparent emasculation, for he also fears that he resembles the women who tortured and abused him: 'Some kind of transmutation had taken place. I had become as monstrous as the women I was looking for. That was their effect, their legacy. Like vam-pires, they had turned me into another version of themselves' (*BR*, 203). It is the penetration of his body, his violation by these women, that renders him 'monstrous' – and, by implication, feminine ('another version of themselves').[9] Although his 'monstrosity' quite easily masquerades as hegemonic masculine behaviour, conventional models of masculinity offer little space in which to explore, experience and negotiate shame.

There is no triumphant ending here, just defeat and the transformation, perhaps, of shame into guilt – but not in any way that could be described as 'heroic' in the sense that Connor writes of. We never learn who the women are or why they kidnapped him. Indeed, the protagonist's promiscuous quest to discover their identities is shown to be self-defeating, diminishing rather than increasing his knowledge, as his memories of their bodies are fatally overlaid with the memories of the many bodies of the women he has since slept with: 'Far from exposing them, as I had thought it might, the process was actually protecting them from exposure. To put it more bluntly, my initiative had the seeds of its own certain failure implanted within it' (*BR*, 205). In fact, it is a process which unwittingly compounds his misery, gifting him a sexually transmitted disease which leaves him feeling (again) 'dirty, ashamed' (*BR*, 205), and ultimately getting him arrested for assault when he 'attacks' a woman in a bar who he thinks might be one of his kidnappers. The ending, then, offers us little in the way of healing or redemption and little sense that shame can be overcome.

What fragile optimism there is, here, lies in the protagonist's realization, as he sits in prison accused of assault and attempted rape, that he 'could sink no further', that he 'had reached a place, at last, some kind of solid ground or bedrock, on which it might be possible to build' (*BR*, 262). But that 'bedrock' – so reassuring a word – is actually a place of absolute debasement, which compels him at last to confess and confront his shame. As the policeman Olsen urges him, 'gently', to 'go back to the beginning', the space opens up in which he might share his experiences, and we are returned (even as the text ends) to the start of the tale, with a circularity ultimately more disconcerting than comforting (*BR*, 264).

The Book of Revelation, as I hope this chapter has demonstrated, is always keenly alert to the more ambivalent feelings bound up with masculine shame: complicity, arousal, anger, bewilderment, self-hatred and occasional, erratic, empowerment. Thomson's protagonist (unlike Amis's) is unquestionably the victim of a horrifying sexual trauma, but his navigation of his own victimhood represents an interrogation rather than a shoring up of his troublesome masculinity; indeed, he moves some way towards acknowledging the more unsettling, identity-undoing 'shame of being a man' that Connor's essay so acutely anatomizes. Moreover, the novel's deceptively simple narratorial, structural and linguistic devices implicitly reflect on the challenges of speaking shame, refusing us the consolations of confession and closure, expiation and overcoming. Alongside and in contradistinction to the work of contemporaries such as Amis, Thomson's more nuanced and disturbing negotiation of shame in *The Book of Revelation* presents it as a state that might be available to men, that might both precede and extend beyond the unusual circumstances of his protagonist's particular experience of shaming, that might challenge our perceptions of masculinity rather than remaining (as in the work of so many of his contemporaries) fundamentally incompatible with it – indeed, the birthright of women.

Notes

1 It is perhaps necessary to distinguish between shame and humiliation, though Silvan Tomkins, in one of the best-known and most cited accounts, places them together as 'shame-humiliation' (as distinct from 'contempt-disgust'): 'Shyness, shame, and guilt are not distinguished from each other at the level of affect, in our view. They are one and the same affect. This is not to say that shyness in the presence of a stranger, shame at a failure to cope successfully with a challenge, and guilt for an immorality are the same experience. Clearly they are not. The conscious awareness of each of these experiences is quite distinct. Yet the affect that we term shame- humiliation, which is a component of each of these total experiences, is one and the same affect' (Tomkins, 1995: 133). Etymologically the words can be distinguished, however: 'shame' has Anglo-Saxon and Germanic origins (Old English, 'sc(e)amu'; modern German, 'Scham'), while 'humiliation' has its roots in the Latin 'humiliare', to 'make low or humble in position, condition, or feeling' (*OED*, online version, December 2013).

2 For an extended account of the significance of Aidos within classical mythology, see Cairns (1993).

3 Freud (1961: 48) refers to shame and disgust as 'watchmen' in *Five Lectures on Psychoanalysis*; Malcolm Pines (2008: 93) summarizes the Freudian view of shame as the 'guardian of morality'.

4 Note, for example, how the editors of *Scenes of Shame* set literature up in contrast to traditional psychoanalytic discourse, as providing 'a privileged place of redress, a sphere of expression where emotional life can be explored and refined in ways that are discouraged elsewhere', claiming that 'in art and literature, shame and repression are diminished, and the richness of emotional life [...] is investigated in its complexity' (Adamson and Clark, 1999: 6, 15).

5 As an illustration of this, see my article on A. M. Homes and Mary Gaitskill, which addresses both their resistance to a redemptive logic and the critical unease that this provokes: Mitchell (2013).

6 These terms appear in the novel's epigraph, which also gives the novel its title, and which is taken from Alexander Herzen's assertion (in the very different context of revolutionary Russian socialism in the nineteenth century) that 'the departing world leaves behind it not an heir, but a pregnant widow. Between the death of one and the birth of the other, much water will flow by, a long night of chaos and desolation will pass' (Amis, 2010: prelims, n.p.). We might note in passing the way this epigraph figures historical change via a (ruined?) female body defined (as widow and mother) solely in relation to male others, and functioning at best as a vehicle for some possible future – what Margaret Atwood (1985: 136) termed, in another context, an 'ambulatory chalice'.

7 Another way to approach this question of whether/how shame can be spoken is to consider Primo Levi's writing on the shame of the Holocaust survivor (see *The Drowned and the Saved* and *If This Is A Man*). As Bewes (2006: 37, emphasis added) explains it: 'Levi's shame is *the shame of being able to speak*, of having the tools to bear witness, and, by that same fact, nothing to bear witness to. It is precisely because one has been spared the horror that one is able to speak of it.'

8 See Sedgwick's comments on 'the childhood scene of shame' in 'Queer Performativity' (1993) and the equivalent chapter in *Touching Feeling* (2003). See also my 'Cleaving to the Scene of Shame'.

9 The use of the term 'monstrous' is suggestive, given its long-standing association with femininity and, in particular, with the maternal body and the anxieties it provokes in a patriarchal society. See, for example: Braidotti (1996); Creed (2000). While the protagonist's thoughts here could be read as reinforcing the 'dread of the generative mother' that Creed (2000: 129) elucidates, constructing the women as vampire mothers, he goes further in seeming to take on the burden of monstrosity himself.

Works Cited

Adamson, Joseph and Hilary Clark (1999) 'Introduction: Shame, Affect, and Writing', in Adamson and Clark (eds) *Scenes of Shame: Psychoanalysis, Shame, and Writing*, pp. 1–34. Albany, NY: SUNY Press.

Agamben, Giorgio (2008) *Remnants of Auschwitz*. New York: Zone Books.

Amis, Martin (2010) *The Pregnant Widow*. London: Vintage.

Atwood, Margaret (1985) *The Handmaid's Tale*. London: Virago.

Bartky, Sandra (1990) *Femininity and Domination*. London: Routledge.

Bewes, Timothy (2006) 'Shame, Ventriloquy, and the Problem of the Cliché in Caryl Phillips', *Cultural Critique* 63: 33–60.

Bewes, Timothy (2011) *The Event of Postcolonial Shame*. Princeton, NJ: Princeton University Press.

Bouson, J. Brooks (2009) *Embodied Shame*. Albany, NY: SUNY Press.

Braidotti, Rosi (1996) 'Signs of Wonder and Traces of Doubt: On Teratology and Embodied Differences', in Nina Lykke and Rosi Braidotti (eds) *Between Monsters, Goddesses and Cyborgs*, pp. 135–52. London: Zed Books.

Cairns, Douglas L. (1993) *Aidos*. Oxford: Clarendon.

Connor, Steven (2000) 'The Shame of Being a Man', URL (consulted May 2012): http://www.stevenconnor.com/shame/

Creed, Barbara (2000) 'Alien and the Monstrous-Feminine', in Gill Kirkup (ed.) *The Gendered Cyborg*, pp. 122–30. London: Routledge.

Deleuze, Gilles (1997) 'Literature and Life', trans. Daniel W. Smith and Michael A. Greco, *Critical Inquiry* 23(2): 225–30.

Fanon, Frantz (1968) *Black Skin, White Masks*, trans. C. Markham. London: MacGibbon & Kee.

Flood, Alison (2009) 'Martin Amis says new novel will get him "in trouble with the feminists"', *Guardian*, Friday 20 November, URL (consulted May 2012): https://www.theguardian.com/books/2009/nov/20/martin-amis-novel-feminists-sister

Freud, Sigmund (1961) *Five Lectures on Psychoanalysis* (48), trans. and ed. James Strachey. New York: Norton.

Halperin David and Valerie Traub (eds) (2009) *Gay Shame*. Chicago, IL: Chicago University Press.

Kaufman, Gershen (1989) *The Psychology of Shame*. New York: Springer.

Koestenbaum, Wayne (2011) *Humiliation*. New York: Picador.

Lawson, Mark (2010) Interview with Martin Amis, *Front Row*, BBC Radio 4, 2 February.

Lea, Daniel and Berthold Schoene (2003) 'Masculinity in Transition: An Introduction', in Daniel Lea and Berthold Schoene (eds) *Posting the Male*, pp7–17. Amsterdam: Rodopi.

Lehtinen, Ullaliina (1998) 'How Does One Know What Shame Is?', *Hypatia* 13(1): 56–77.

Levi, Primo (1979) *If This Is A Man*, trans. Stuart Woolf. London: Abacus.

Levi, Primo (1988) *The Drowned and The Saved*, trans. Raymond Rosenthal. London: Abacus.

Leys, Ruth (2007) *From Guilt to Shame*. Princeton, NJ: Princeton University Press.

Long, Camilla (2010) 'Martin Amis and the sex war', *The Times*, 24 January, URL (consulted May 2012): http://www.thesundaytimes.co.uk/sto/culture/books/article195426.ece

Love, Heather (2007) *Feeling Backward*. Cambridge, MA: Harvard University Press.

Manion, Jennifer C. (2003) 'Girls Blush, Sometimes: Gender, Moral Agency, and the Problem of Shame', *Hypatia* 18(3): 21–41.

McEwan, Ian (2007) *On Chesil Beach*. London: Vintage.

Mitchell, Kaye (2013) 'Cleaving to the Scene of Shame: Stigmatized Childhoods in *The End of Alice* and *Two Girls, Fat and Thin*', *Contemporary Women's Writing* 7(3): 309–27.

Morgan, Michael L. (2008) *On Shame*. London: Routledge.

Munt, Sally (2007) *Queer Attachments*. Aldershot: Ashgate.

Nathanson, Donald L. (ed.) (1988) *The Many Faces of Shame*. New York: Guilford.

Nathanson, Donald L. (1992) *Shame and Pride: Affect, Sex and the Birth of the Self*. New York: Norton.

Nussbaum, Martha (2004) *Hiding from Humanity: Disgust, Shame and the Law*. Princeton, NJ: Princeton University Press.

Oxford English Dictionary, Second Edition (1989). Oxford: Oxford University Press. [Online version, consulted July 2014].

Pines, Malcolm (2008) 'Shame: What Psychoanalysis Does and Does Not Say', in Claire Pajaczkowska and Ivan Ward (eds) *Shame and Sexuality: Psychoanalysis and Visual Culture*, pp. 93–106. London: Routledge.

Probyn, Elspeth (2005) *Blush: Faces of Shame*. Minneapolis: Minnesota University Press.

Roth, Philip (2007) *Exit Ghost*. Boston, MA: Houghton Mifflin.

Roth, Philip (2009) *The Humbling*. Boston, MA: Houghton Mifflin.

Sartre, Jean-Paul (1958) *Being and Nothingness*, trans. Hazel E. Barnes. London: Methuen.

Sedgwick, Eve Kosofsky (1993) 'Queer Performativity: Henry James's *The Art of the Novel*', *GLQ* 1(1): 1–16.

Sedgwick, Eve Kosofsky, (2003) *Touching Feeling*. Durham, NC: Duke University Press.

Segal, Lynne (2001) 'Back to the boys? Temptations of the good gender theorist', *Textual Practice* 15(2): 231–50.

Taylor, Gabriele (1985) *Pride, Shame, and Guilt*. Oxford: Clarendon.

Tomkins, Silvan (1995) 'Shame-Humiliation and Contempt-Disgust', in Eve Kosofsky Sedgwick and Adam Franks (eds) *Shame and Its Sisters: A Silvan Tomkins Reader*, pp. 133–78. Durham, NC: Duke University Press.

Williams, Bernard (1993) *Shame and Necessity*. Berkeley: University of California Press.

Something's Not Quite Right
Atmosphere in *The Insult*

Rebecca Pohl

The knowledge problem

The opening passage of Rupert Thomson's 1996 novel *The Insult* is characterized by an apparent tension between certainty of subject and uncertainty of situation. The novel's opening plunges into circumstances already underway, the emphatic first-person narrator the only immediate anchor:

> 'You've been shot.'
> I heard someone say it. I wouldn't have known otherwise; I wouldn't have realised. All I could remember was four tomatoes – three of them motionless, one still rolling. And a black shape, too. A shape that had a curve to it.
> *I've been shot.*
> Sirens circled me like ghosts.
> I slipped away, the feeling of having fallen from a plane, of falling through dark air, and the plane flying on without me …
> Each time I woke up, it was night.
> Then voices spoke to me, out of nothing. Voices told me the rest. You'd been shopping, they said. (*I*, 3)

Characters haunted by uncertainty are a trope in Thomson's writing beginning with his debut novel *Dreams of Leaving* (1987) where Moses can never quite shake the sensation of feeling awkward and out of place. Glade in *Soft!* (1998) remains completely unaware that she has been cognitively manipulated by a large drinks corporation now intent on covering up the scandal by assassinating her, but feels disconnected from her friends and self. *The Book of Revelation* (1999) begins with the main character waking from having been drugged and kidnapped to find '[h]is eyes didn't work properly. Things spun round, tilted, misted over' (*BR*, 11). In all three cases, uncertainty is linked to a problem of perception which leaves the characters feeling decontextualized and displaced. *The Insult*'s narrator, in the passage quoted above, is also out of place. The repetition of 'I' at the beginning of a series of sentences and clauses emphasizes the subject position which can be inhabited with enough certainty to lay claim to that 'I'. At the same time, this beginning is distinctly after the fact, referencing a past event that itself remains indistinct: 'a black shape'. No context is provided at this point, or at any point in the novel; the full extent of the explanation of the situation is the straightforward assertion of fact, issued from an indistinct source: 'You've been shot.' Although the 'I' seems so emphatically present in this passage, the first word of the text is 'you' setting up the separation of subject and object. The declaration is issued by an outside voice, yet is fully adopted by the first-person narrator. From the very start then the text demands that the voice of authority, which is providing the perspective, be interrogated. More than that, this external, disembodied authority ('someone', 'voices', 'they') states what has happened to the narrator. This is necessary because, as also becomes clear in this passage, the I-narrator is far less certain of the situation than he is of his subject position. He is preoccupied with cognitive processes of understanding ('known', 'realized', 'remember'), or more specifically, with his failure to achieve knowledge, realization and memory without outside help. The internal narration is initiated from outside, the subject explained, indeed enabled, by somebody outside the self. The certainty of subject pretended by the narrator's repetition of 'I' is hence shown to be unstable even as it asserts itself – it is displaced. The italicized quotation 'I've been shot' further destabilizes the subject position, the italics distancing the statement from the narrator's preceding and subsequent thoughts, not quite owning the phrase that will come to determine his subject position. In fact, the 'I' then 'slip[s] away', the subject position far less securely anchored than the prominence of the pronoun might initially suggest.

It is this slipperiness, the unavailability of certainty, that I focus on in this chapter. The text here poses a knowledge problem: knowledge of what has happened, knowledge of self, and then increasingly knowledge of what is happening. The narration is retrospective, and, crucially, it shifts into the past conditional ('wouldn't have') suggesting that the narrator is speaking from a future position of knowledge and understanding which makes the story cohere. But this position of certitude is based on that opening line, issuing from an undisclosed source, itself indistinct, so that the subject relies entirely on that external position for his own position, his own knowledge. And the situation that begins the novel is no more distinct than its provenance: it is dark, night-time; it feels ghostly and the narrator is asleep or unconscious during much of it, unable to make sense of things so that 'voices' speak to him 'out of nothing', out of context. The knowledge at play in this particular scene is thus rendered unreliable as the narrator undercuts his own certainty regarding the nature of his knowledge. As the way into the novel, it colours *The Insult* as a whole. From the start, a feeling of uncertainty, or put differently an atmosphere of doubt, pervades the text: something is not quite right.

That 'something is not quite right' is an aspect of Thomson's writing that is frequently picked up on by reviewers. Two terms repeated across reviews of all his novels are 'unease' and 'unsettling' (Campbell-Johnston, 1998; Clark, 2007; Koning, 1999; Myerson, 2010; Merritt, 2013; Thompson, 2007). Richard Davenport-Hines, for instance, speaks of 'the hallucinatory menace of Thomson's novels' in his review of *The Insult*, and in her review of *Secrecy* Stephanie Merritt remarks, 'Through all his fiction, so wildly different on the surface, runs a unifying thread of the macabre, a haunting, dream-like dissociation from reality' (Davenport-Hines, 1996: 24; Merritt, 2013). But the reviews also habitually highlight the eclecticism of Thomson's oeuvre:

dystopian fictions, historical novels, thrillers, crime fictions, none of which fully conform to the genres they invoke. This disparity between texts is both celebrated and lamented, and is frequently cited as a comprehensive description of the oeuvre that itself purportedly lacks cohesion (Neilan, 2009; Wroe, 2013). In this context, 'eclectic' operates as a sort of shorthand descriptor that assumes familiarity with the writing, and it has turned into a critical commonplace. But as John McAuliffe shows in his chapter in this collection, continuities can be traced across Thomson's texts through analysing intertextuality. I am interested in another aspect of the texts that reveals continuity across works, and I am calling it atmosphere. Despite the habitual verdict of eclecticism, most existent Thomson criticism agrees on the fact that it is sinister, surreal, strange, that the texts produce haunting and disturbing effects. This chapter will begin to unravel the textual processes that produce these feelings and show how reading atmosphere makes them available for critical analysis. My reading of atmosphere as a crucial category for thinking about Thomson's writing builds on Sianne Ngai's treatment of the concept of tone. Ngai's work is helpful here because she foregrounds the importance to tone of an idea of totality while proposing an analytical framework by which to approach it. Historically, tone, too, has signified cohesion: 'tone usually refers precisely to those aspects of written language that are neither lexical nor syntactical, but that appear, at least at first, somewhat intangibly, as a quality of the text as a whole, or of a significant part of it' (Greene, et al., 2012: 1441). Ngai reclaims tone from what she terms its 'threat of a "soft" impressionism' – its 'intangibility' – to show how it is a productive category for the analysis of 'compressed assessments of complex "situations," for indicating the *total* [sic] web of relations' at play (Ngai, 2005: 42). Emphasizing tone as holistic and as totalizing, she nevertheless redefines it as 'a global and hyperrelational concept of feeling that encompasses attitude: a literary text's affective bearing, orientation, or "set toward" its audience and world' (Ngai, 2005: 43). So while the totality is crucial, it is composed of multiple relations and these can be available for analysis. Ngai's reading shows how tone relies on the affective, and how analysis of its affective aspects is both necessary and potentially enabling for a critique of ideology. I suggest here that atmosphere offers similar possibilities and poses similar challenges, and can help to work through some of the 'singular' qualities of Thomson's writing. Unpicking what appears to be a complex totality coincides with tracing ideological attachments. In the case of Thomson's *The Insult* that attachment is a critique of knowledge formation grounded in stable subject positions.[1]

The opening section of *The Insult* is uneasy and unsettled, neither the narrating subject position nor the situation he finds himself in can be easily made sense of, and the quick acceptance of the given explanation by the narrator, who is clearly not fully compos menti, sets up an atmosphere of unreliability from early on. This remains a central concern throughout the novel. The random act of violence that initiates the narrative leaves the narrator Martin Blom fully blind, but he soon begins to explore the hospital grounds, where he claims to regain the experience of sight (*I*, 17). Obsessed with his new-found vision, Blom sleeps during the day and walks about first the hospital and then a series of cities at night, in the dark when he says his vision returns. This miracle of sorts, the return even of night-time vision after the optical nerve – according to the medics' diagnosis – has been violently severed, is questioned by the insistently disbelieving voice of his neurosurgeon. Dr Visser warns the narrator early on that 'people who suffer from cortical blindness often believe, despite proof to the contrary, that they can see' and that he 'might also experience visual hallucinations' (*I*, 7). As it turns out, this throw-away remark punctures the subsequent narration, casting doubt over the narrator's interpretations of events and people, and making it uncertain whether, for example, the random sex scenes he goes on to describe at the Hotel Kosminsky 'really' happen. Blom himself also casts uncertainty over the narrative early on when he recounts one of his recurrent anxiety dreams, where his body flies to pieces only slowly reassembling upon waking: 'And there were parts of me that didn't reappear, of course. [...] My eyesight, too. That never came back either' (*I*, 6). Precisely because it is not entirely clear whether he is referring to his eyesight in the context of his dream or in the 'real' world, Blom here subtly undermines his own subsequent narrative.

In a reunion with Dr Visser this unreliability is made explicit without being resolved as it remains unclear whether Visser is manipulating the narrator. The physician asks Blom to describe something to prove his night vision and Blom chooses the doctor himself:

> I sat back and looked at him. Where should I begin? Not the moustache. Too obvious.
> 'Well, let's see,' I said. 'There's your shoes. They've got metal on them.'
> 'You can hear that.'
> 'Just testing.' I smiled. 'Testing your alertness. Your shoes are black –'
> 'They're not black.'
> 'They're such a dark brown, I thought they were black.'
> 'What else?'
> 'Your hair,' I said. 'It's brown.'
> 'You knew that already. I told you, in the clinic.'
> 'All right.' I stayed calm. 'Your face, then. Let's start with your moustache – '
> 'I don't have a moustache.'
> I stared at Visser in disbelief. 'But I'm looking right at it.'
> 'You're imagining it,' he said. 'The moustache is an illusion. It's part of the imaginary picture you've built up.' (*I*, 224–5)

Up until this point, there has been no direct challenge to Blom's night vision, so that the first-person narration has established itself as certain and secure despite the ambiguous opening section. But here, when he is confronted with an external perspective that explicitly contradicts his descriptions, that security is unsettled. Each time Blom gets a detail wrong, he immediately explains why he did, and the text never resolves which of the two men is lying. This passage of direct dialogue is increasingly tense, beginning with what look like excuses made by Blom for getting things wrong: the first visual detail he lists, the metal soles, is shown up for being auditory (and redefined as a 'test' of Visser's own perceptiveness); the second, the colour of the shoes, is explained away as a nearly pedantic insistence on precision of degree which the doctor neither affirms nor contradicts. When it comes to Visser's facial appearance, this is already known to Blom from their first meeting in the hospital: "'My name's Visser. Bruno Visser.' "What do you look like?" I said. "An understandable question." He mentioned light-brown hair, pale-blue eyes' (*I*, 5). Even in this first meeting there is something odd about Visser's manner – it is enigmatic, authoritative, and it prefigures the tussle over control that takes place in their later reunion. When Blom asks about his own appearance the doctor 'paused, his silence awkward – or perhaps just curious, intrigued' (*I*, 5). The narrator is describing an atmosphere *in the room* (awkward silence), but is also immediately offering an alternative interpretation ('curious', 'intrigued') that begins to suggest an agenda. Like the atmosphere in the hospital room, atmosphere in the novel is determined by uncertainty that shades into paranoia about motives, authority, control. It is this same uncertainty that determines Blom's mood in the later scene where he shifts from being calm to being furious, regarding Visser as 'trying to undermine me, establish control' (*I*, 225). And it is also the same uncertainty the text is foregrounding about Blom's perspective, newly blind and recently traumatized, guiding the narrative of the whole novel. This feeling of uncertainty and the clash of perspectives are reinforced when Blom's final attempt at describing a visual detail is flat out denied by Visser, who now in turn explains away the moustache as a visual illusion. Nevertheless, the text does not easily settle into either reliable or unreliable narration, instead sustaining the slipperiness of the situation – the fact of Visser's moustache is never resolved. This is one of those hallucinatory moments, an example of the 'dissociation from reality' Merritt picks out. The text here is pervaded by and produces an atmosphere of paranoia: the narrator is increasingly paranoid and this is figured in his narration, which constitutes the text. In other words, something is not quite right, or more specifically, something doesn't *feel* quite right.

Contextualizing atmosphere

It is the notion of 'not quite right' that I want to probe further, as a quality that is characteristic of Thomson's writing not only in *The In-*

sult, but in his wider oeuvre. This is the quality that Boyd Tonkin is referring to when he notes 'the singular climate of Thomson's novels' (Tonkin, 2010). Tonkin's observation, in a review of Thomson's memoir *This Party's Got to Stop*, suggests that some quality persists through Thomson's oeuvre as a whole: the 'singular' quality is taken to encompass a generality, even a totality. And the name he gives to that quality is 'climate'. Elsewhere Tonkin writes: 'The moment you open the door into any of Rupert Thomson's eerie and hypnotic fictions, the everyday world slides [...] and [you encounter an] unsettling climate of mystery, peril and enchantment' (Tonkin, 2005). Paul Tilzey in turn notes how 'the terrible aridity of the climate seem[s] to have affected the tone of the book in some insidious way' in *Air and Fire* (Tilzey, 1993). Climate implies both weather conditions and affective conditions, and it refers to a general sense rather than a specific one. Thomson's writing seems to invite such a holistic reading that attends to feeling.

In Tilzey's review, geographical 'climate' translates into textual 'tone'. But climate is perhaps more closely related to another term with a long history in literary criticism: atmosphere. Like climate, atmosphere implies an extensive quality extending throughout a text, for example, or across an oeuvre, and it seems to be recognizable without necessarily being graspable. In this sense, atmosphere can appear both vague, hard to pin down, and simultaneously self-evident. These tendencies contribute to a prevailing critical orthodoxy concerning atmosphere, epitomized in the *Routledge Dictionary of Literary Terms* entry: 'A vague term with diminishing currency, atmosphere is employed where the overtones of the words and ideas employed reinforce one another' (Childs and Fowler, 2006: 11). The 'diminishing currency' of atmosphere in English literary studies can be traced to some of the early and influential formalist criticism that shaped the field. William Empson quips in *Seven Types of Ambiguity*: 'if it is said that the verbal analyst is a crude irrelevant fellow who should be thinking about the atmosphere, the reply is that though there may be an atmosphere to which analysis is irrelevant, it is not necessarily anything very respectable' (Empson, 2004: 21). Empson too, is suggesting that atmosphere is a suspect term unavailable for critical reading, that it is 'no assembly of grammatical meanings, capable of analysis' (Empson, 2004: 17). For Empson, the challenge is to show that formalist analysis is just as important to meaning as is the elusive atmosphere, which is linked with taste, discernment and immanence. But crucially, he does not finally dismiss atmosphere, enjoining that 'it is very necessary for the critic to remember about the atmosphere', precisely because formalist analysis, too, is concerned with the totality of the poem even as it zooms in on those specific 'grammatical meanings' (Empson, 2004: 17). As Empson recognizes, this elusive quality cannot simply be ignored, precisely because it returns criticism to the sense of totality which formalist analysis pushes against.

Although atmosphere has tended to disappear from critical vocabularies in English literary studies, or be considered vague and outmoded, it has a long history in aesthetics, not least in its form as one of the words by which *Stimmung* has been translated. There has been a resurgence of interest in the concept of *Stimmung* in the German-speaking academy where recent publications in comparative literature and the history of philosophy have begun to explore the richness of the category (e.g. Arburg and Rickenbacher, 2012; Gisbertz, 2009). Hans Ulrich Gumbrecht's 2012 book *Atmosphere, Mood, Stimmung*, translated from the German by Erik Butler and published by Stanford University Press, is a prominent instance of this interest being carried over into English. According to Anna Katharina Gisbertz, the renewed interest in German scholarship is due to the rise of affect theory, where *Stimmung* shows a striking similarity to the current discourses surrounding affect. The cited reviews of Thomson's novels, with their focus on 'climate' and the 'sinister' tie in with this focus. In his foundational piece on *Stimmung* for the *Historisches Wörterbuch Ästhetischer Grundbegriffe*, Germanist David Wellbery offers a comprehensive overview of the historical development of the term, including close attention to semantic and etymological as well as contextual detail. Wellbery concludes that *Stimmung* is resistant but also intriguing to analysis and links this apparent paradox to an issue raised by an analysis of the term itself. He argues that it cannot be tied into the conventional philosophical binary of objective and subjective: *Stimmung* can describe a room or a landscape, and it can describe a person's state of being; more than that, it also describes the interrelation between subject and object. The indeterminate location of subjectivity, which oscillates between positions of interiority and exteriority in *The Insult's* opening section, for example, creates an atmosphere of uncertainty and unease precisely because that binary is radically troubled. A brief discussion of the three common translations of *Stimmung* – Gumbrecht speaks of translation 'clusters' (Gumbrecht, 2012: 3) – will demonstrate the richness contained in the German and go some way towards unravelling its value for thinking about Thomson's work. *Stimmung* has been variously translated into English as mood, attunement, and atmosphere. As with any translation, especially of a term as complexly metaphoric as *Stimmung*, these variants create gaps, and it is tempting to conclude that the term is simply untranslatable. But rather than resigning to the failure of translation, I want to investigate these gaps a little further to show how they are instructive and enable a discussion of *Stimmung* in literature, in English. The concept of *Stimmung*, especially its translation as atmosphere, in turn allows a reading of Thomson's writing that accounts for dissonance without despairing at its eclecticism.

One translation of *Stimmung* is mood, and it is as mood that the concept has returned into Anglophone critical theory, with two special issues dedicated to the topic since 2012 (Felski and Fraiman, 2012; Highmore and Bourne Taylor, 2014). As Rita Felski and Susan Fraiman point out in their introduction to the *New Literary History* special issue, mood as a critical term gains currency in the context of affect studies because it, too, relates to emotion. Following the work of René Rosfort and Giovanni Stanghellini, Felski and Fraiman argue that unlike emotion '[m]oods are usually described as ambient, vague, diffuse, hazy, and intangible' and that, unlike affect, mood 'lingers, tarries, settles in, accumulates, sticks around' (Felski and Fraiman, 2012: v). This taxonomy suggests that the main difference between the terms is a scale of increasing duration – from emotion to affect to mood – where increasing duration also leads to increasing 'diffus[ion]', or 'intangibility'. This temporal extension correlates with increasing physical or spatial non-specificity: emotion is brief and locatable in the subject (it is personal), affect takes longer and flows between elements, and mood finally signifies even more broad-ly, describing space rather than place. As demonstrated by Felski and Fraiman's proposed definition, however, these distinctions can only ever be preliminary; there is considerable overlap between the three. One such overlap is the term 'sticky', which is crucial to Sara Ahmed's discussion of affective economies. Ahmed contends that affect moves sideways across objects by sticking to them (or firmly attaching) and then sticking them together (binding objects) to generate the illusion of cohesion (Ahmed, 2004). Felski and Fraiman invoke the same term, but change the proposition. Now, affect is not something that *sticks to*, but mood is something that *sticks around*. The preposition has rendered the term both spatial and non-specific.

In addition to the relation of degrees, mood, according to Felski and Fraiman, is qualitatively distinct from both affect and emotion, and it is here that it becomes especially fruitful as an analytic tool to them. Mood, they argue, troubles the opposition between feeling and thought that much of the foundational writing in affect theory high-lights (e.g. Grossberg 1992; Massumi, 2002). In fact, mood specifi-cally relates affect to thought: 'the power of moods [is] to shape what we perceive, feel, and believe; to structure the way we comprehend and reason as well as act' (Felski and Fraiman, 2012: ix). Or as Ben Highmore and Jenny Bourne Taylor put it, mood is 'how the social and cultural world is lived as qualities and forms, as sense and feel-ing. It is how the world enlivens us and flattens us.' (Highmore and Bourne Taylor, 2014: 9) Mood, then, offers a translation of *Stimmung* that accounts for the subject- and object-specific signification of the German term, as well as tying it in to an existing critical discussion, and it accounts for the durational and the non-specific. Hence why, in *Five Gates of Hell*, the 'apocalyptic mood' is one of the text's lingering effects (Gooderham, 1991).

What mood does not account for is the strong musical connota-tion of *Stimmung*. It is this aspect that helps unpack the phrase *hier stimmt etwas nicht*, which corresponds in translation to the 'some-thing's not quite right' that attaches to so much of Thomson's writing. This musical facet is captured in another common translation of *Stim-mung*: attunement. Attunement brings the tonal to bear on mood, and is often used for translating Heidegger's notion of *Stimmung* (see Ngai above). Attunement hence, also, picks up on the intimate connection between feeling and thought, signifying in much the same way as mood. What attunement draws out that is not quite captured by mood, is the importance of relations to *Stimmung*: things can be in tune or out of tune, they can resonate harmoniously or jar in disharmony. Though cumbersome, attunement is a crucial translation of *Stimmung*, insisting on both the particular and the whole, insisting on the relationality at the heart of the concept. It is attunement that Highfield and Bourne Taylor (2014: 6) draw on when they speak of mood as 'an orchestration of many factors'. Like an orchestra, *Stimmung* involves a number of discrete elements that, in the first instance, might appear inseparable from the whole, might appear to resonate only together, as a totality. As Empson points out in the context of his discussion of atmosphere, music can be both sensed and analysed (Empson, 2004: 16–17) – the vagueness and diffusion ascribed to mood is hence complicated by the idea of attunement. Attunement also offers a language to speak about those moments where the parts do not quite seem to assemble into a whole, or at least not a whole that rings harmoniously: where something is out of tune – *etwas stimmt nicht* – something is not quite right. The forms of knowledge at the beginning of *The Insult* resist coming together in any harmony and the sense of uncertainty and paranoia is an effect of this dissonance.

To return to my starting point, the final common translation of *Stimmung* into English is atmosphere. Atmosphere can also seem to tend towards the 'soft impressionism' Ngai identifies in the critical history of tone, and we have already seen how it has been characterized by contemporary texts on literary criticism as vague and diffuse. But atmosphere has an additional set of associations that make it especially appropriate for thinking about the 'climate' of Thomson's novels: far more than tone, mood or attunement, atmosphere is a spatial concept. In *The Insult* space is crucial to the narrative as the first-person narrator experiences his loss of control – and his paranoid attempts at regaining control – in and through the negotiation of space. In the way 'mood' has been characterized above, it is associated with an attempt to account for effects that refuse to be localized. Thomson's writing persistently unsettles localization of any kind, be it the localization of knowledge, of perspective, or of place. Blom's narration, for example, attaches definite articles to non-specific, even generic, places throughout the text, foregrounding the tension between the tangible and the intangible through spatial terms (e.g. 'the capital' (*I*, 45); 'the river' (*I*, 45), 'Central Station' (*I*, 59); 'the red-light district, behind the train station' (*I*, 60); 'the city' (*I*, 245); 'the far north-east of the country' (*I*, 246)). Atmosphere hence comes to seem an especially appropriate way of thinking about the text because it accounts for space. I want to suggest, in parallel to Ngai, that atmosphere, while at first sight appearing to operate as a diffuse whole, is constituted by relations and there are moments where it becomes available for analysis through these relations. These relations can be out of joint, or out of tune, and it is perhaps here that they become most readily available for critical analysis and perform the work of resistance to easy comprehensibility and comprehensiveness that characterizes Thomson's writing.

Hier stimmt etwas nicht, 'something is not quite right', means that the relations are off kilter, are not in tune, not in concert. The knowledge problem at the beginning of *The Insult* can be described as one of misalignment, where the knowledge of the first-person narrator does not map onto the patterns at play. Similar uncertainties pervade Blom's perceptions throughout the novel, for example at his first view of Loots, who will go on to become his companion of sorts. Blom catches sight of a man wearing a bright acrobat's leotard riding his bicycle whilst doing a handstand and juggling oranges with his feet. Blom applauds at the end of the performance, but Loots, without acknowledgement, simply cycles on, and a passer-by wonders what Blom is applauding (*I*, 74). This brief scene explicitly echoes information Blom has previously been told about Loots: that he used to work in a circus and likes to cycle. It is extraordinary in its challenge to physics and fundamentally put into question by the passer-by, rendering the situation comedic, even surreal. A short scene in Blom's family home achieves a similar effect: 'Reaching for my wineglass, I knocked it over. Deliberately' (*I*, 46). The addition of intention to a clichéd act of clumsiness, especially when that intention is presented as an afterthought, suggests its rationalization after the fact and puts that intention into question even as it articulates it. It also inflects the general atmosphere of unease, of being out of place, with humour. This nuance of humour is important to the way atmosphere means in the novel. Though perhaps leaving an overall impression, atmosphere is not necessarily a totality, not only because it is constituted by relations, but also because it can be disrupted. In the scenes described above, the slight but sudden shift into the comedic disrupts the pervasive atmosphere of unease and paranoia. But this shift also still works through the knowledge problem because the scenes cannot be resolved as either absurd imaginings or faithful accounts and thus further trouble the reliability of the narration. The atmosphere of unease and unsettledness is one where the 'orchestration' does not resolve into a harmonious whole, but where discord is foregrounded and these moments of humour also work towards that: uncertainty, in the text, does not have a unified tone.

Reading atmosphere

I have already shown how atmosphere works in a particular moment in the close readings that began this chapter. I will now take a longer view, to begin to approach the totality that seems so important to atmosphere, and I will do this by foregrounding space. Early in the text, Blom's nurse at the hospital, Nurse Janssen, attempts to make conversation with Blom by remarking on the 'three beautiful trees' outside his window (*I*, 13), which he derides. But this moment becomes significant just a little while later when Blom is wandering the hospital grounds in the dark and 'realizes' that he can see. This is what he sees:

> The shapes in the green were trees. And I could see the lawn, too, reaching away from me, then sloping down. There was a smoothness at the end of it. A lake. I could see a stand of poplars tapering like rockets as they lifted into the sky. The sky! (*I*, 17)

Landscape, and in particular trees, become crucial markers of sight for Blom, and are often the site of juxtaposition, again ringing out of tune.

Trees, and woods, return throughout the text most often constituting moments of unstable knowledge. As Blom is increasingly convinced that Visser is stalking him, he at one point dreads looking out of his hotel window for fear of seeing '[t]hree beautiful trees' (*I*, 194) – a throwback to his hospital room. This discrete moment works to trouble the totality of the preceding narrative because it casts doubt on Blom's reliability: what Blom says he sees mirrors the prior description by the nurse. When Visser visits Blom in the latter's hometown the two men conclude their meeting with a walk in the 'cool evening':

> Fog had drifted across the town; the light around the street-lamps was soft and round, the density of candy-floss. Across the road from the café was a wooded area. I suggested a stroll. To my surprise Visser agreed.
> We walked in silence for a while, pine needles snapping beneath our feet. Light flashed through the gloom in a flat, blue arc: a jay. (*I*, 52)

The overall atmosphere here is crystallized *in* but not contained *by* the 'gloom'. Gloom describes the atmosphere, but is also only one element of it. The scene takes place in the evening, it is foggy, which renders the light diffuse; it is silent, again an effect of the fog that mutes both light and sound. By taking place among trees, specifically pine trees, this section is tied back to that earlier moment in the text, when Blom first 'sees'. His vision is troubled in multiple ways here, then: by the fog, by the trees, and by the reference to an earlier moment of uncertain authority. This tying back is a movement from the particular to the whole. It is through repeated references such as the trees that the totality of atmosphere is produced in the text. The reiterations are threaded throughout the novel, producing the impression of an overall atmosphere, from the hospital grounds to the wooded mountains Blom escapes to when his paranoia overwhelms him. All the various instances of trees become meaningful when taken together, they form a totality, and they gain meaning in relation to other aspects of the text, for instance the knowledge problem. The first things Blom can see, the things that show him he can see, are trees. Simultaneously, trees recur in moments of uncertainty, they render sight, knowledge, and orientation problematic. The trees represent as much as they obscure or disrupt vision and knowledge. When Blom loses his way on an extended walk whilst staying in the mountains, he gets lost in a landscape of '[o]nly trees huddled in a grove and a dark cold sky above' (*I*, 246). As his anxiety grows, he fixes on blinking lights to guide him to safety only to be completely disoriented by his choice. While he actively decides to walk towards the lights, he also questions their reality and provenance. His doubt renders the situation even more uncertain: 'I thought it had to be the trees between us, shifting in the wind' (*I*, 249). The trees explain the lights he sees, even as they are taken to cause the disruption of his vision, and hence his knowledge. Landscape is shown to be incomprehensible and this manifests in Blom's movement, and failure of movement, travelling through it. Atmosphere is produced in the shifts between subject and surroundings rather than being a steady, a priori setting or background for the subject. In Thomson's novel these shifts create a knowledge problem, they create discordance that is repeated throughout the text. The particular mood that 'settles' through these repetitions into an effect of totality is one of unease, so precisely not one of settling, but of being in tension. If Gumbrecht is right in asserting that 'such tones, atmospheres, and *Stimmungen* never exist wholly independent of the material components of works – above all, their prosody' (Gumbrecht, 2012: 5), then these trees and landscapes contribute towards the unsettled atmosphere of *The Insult*.

Stillness into movement: threat

Another way of framing the previous analysis of trees in the novel is as a reading of landscape. Thomson's knack for writing landscape is picked up by Davenport-Hines in his review of *The Insult*: 'He is a master of minatory landscape and architecture and he always brings a spare, edgy modernity to his scenery' (Davenport-Hines, 1996: 24). Landscape tends to be a matter of descriptive writing in that it is laid out on the page in realist detail, and as the previous readings have demonstrated, it is a writing of space that depends on atmosphere, and one which invokes the affective as well as the spatial. Davenport-Hines qualifies the landscape in Thomson's novel as 'minatory', or threatening, reinforcing this connection and giving a name to one aspect of the book's atmosphere. However, as I have shown in my readings of the conversations between Blom and Visser, threat is not only an effect of description but can also be produced in direct dialogue without commentary or explanation. As Gumbrecht maintains, '[w]ithout exception, all elements comprising texts can contribute to the production of atmospheres and moods, and this means that works rich in *Stimmmung* need not be primarily – and certainly not exclusively – descriptive in nature' (Gumbrecht, 2012: 5). As well as descriptive, the tree passages cited above are concerned with movement: they offer a setting or a background that can be described, a locatable place; at the same time they lend that particular space its atmosphere of uncertainty and threat, through the difficulties of Blom's movement through it. The following passage shows how the characteristic threat (the 'minatory') is produced elsewhere in the text:

> An empty corridor confronted me, all cream walls and gleaming lino-leum. It stretched away into the distance. It stretched so far, I couldn't see an end to it.
> I began to walk.
> Silence. Only the trees shifting beyond the narrow windows and the tinkering of fluorescent lights. Something about the stillness unsettled me. It seemed to be constantly on the verge of becoming movement. It was like the stillness in horror films – stillness as anticipation, stillness as the prelude to a shock. [...] Out of the corner of my eye I saw a movement, something white and quick, but when I turned it was gone. A trapped bird, maybe, or dust in the moonlight.
> (*I*, 31–3)

Blom is on one of his night-time strolls through the hospital which is here figured as an endless corridor, so spatially, and is described in terms of colours and light, so visually. Crucially, though, despite his use of visual perception to describe the space, Blom cannot see its end. This is an enormous space, but it is also an oppressive space, with its glaring fluorescent lights, the eternally repeating cream walls, and the silencing linoleum. The quality foregrounded here is 'silence', though crucially, it is subsequently figured as 'stillness', which combines the absence of sound with the absence of movement. This slipping between modes of perception is echoed in the 'shifting' trees (again) and the 'tinkering' lights: both terms suggest sound as well as movement, unsettling the origin of Blom's judgement, making it unclear whether he is seeing or hearing these things. Stillness here is qualified: it is the kind of stillness 'on the verge of becoming movement'. But there is no agent, the repeated 'it' refers to the stillness itself: it is the determining force and it cannot be controlled. That is why, alongside the explicit invocation of horror films and shock, the passage suggests a kind of threat that is not fixed to discrete elements, and which in this sense, through its repetitions, produces the kind of atmosphere that Davenport-Hines describes as 'minatory': Blom cannot fully grasp the situation, which is here figured as his surroundings, and this causes him anxiety. When the movement that might offer a release of tension finally arrives, it is immediately undercut by a hesitation ('maybe') and by the abrupt shift from the concrete 'trapped bird' to the diffused 'dust'. The building of tension, a particular tautness of relations, repeats throughout the text and is frequently the consequence of discord between the elements of a situation, be they persons or spaces.

The scene in the hospital corridor does indeed turn out to be the prelude to a shock, validating Blom's anxiety: he falls down a flight of stairs and knocks himself unconscious. Though convinced that he knows where he is going, this fall suggests that Blom's orientation – which in his narration is presented with such certainty, except at those crucial moments where it is contradicted – was not aligned with the space. This issue of orientation, where Blom insists on knowing the path only to be confronted by an unknown and, as here, perilous other space, repeats throughout the novel. Later, he acknowledges this: 'I'd learned [...] to orient myself' (*I*, 51). This makes sense because as a newly blind man, he needs to learn new ways of moving in and through space, of perceiving space, and of feeling space. But it also draws out the importance of orientation for successfully moving through and *knowing* space. One of the reasons why the hospital corridor is threatening is because Blom cannot orientate himself so that he does not know which path to follow and ends up in an accident that causes him physical damage (he tastes blood) and also unsettles his knowledge of his surroundings. Moving through space is difficult for him because he has 'no sense of ease or familiarity' (*I*, 47). When he finally sets off on his own, he states: 'I took a deep breath and then hesitated, uncertain which way to turn' (*I*: 59). Blom's disorientation disorients the text: he does not know which way he is facing and so cannot entirely make sense of space or relations and this is where the threat resides. It is through Blom's senses that the reader encounters the world of the novel, and Blom's apparent conviction in the trust-worthiness of these senses is repeatedly cast into question without ever being settled. This means that both his mishaps (which make him seem deluded, comical or overconfident) and his developing paranoia are drawn into a pervasive sense of uncertainty that does not allow the atmosphere of threat to dissipate.

Conclusion

In an interview with *The Times*, Thomson stated that he tends to re-member his own favourite books as 'an atmosphere, a colour or smell' (Crampton, 2000). The affective power of memory is brought to the fore here, as is the intimate relationship between text, *Stimmung* and the spatial. Thomson's interviewer proceeds to attest that, perhaps unsurprisingly, 'Thomson's gift is for atmosphere rather than analy-sis' because he privileges 'texture rather than text' (Crampton, 2000). Texture emphasizes the complex interweaving of strands of meaning, in other words, it emphasizes the relationality of text, and the nov-el. While atmosphere stands in for a whole, for the impression left behind, this impression is shaped by various elements that resonate together. In *The Insult*, this texture is one of unease. From the out-set something 'is not quite right'. This 'something' refers to a holistic impression whose constituent relations become available through an analysis of knowledge economies and space. This is where the diffuse feelings of unease and threat that I have called atmosphere are created. The elements at play in atmosphere cannot easily be assembled into a coherent whole that can then be contained in the process of knowing. In places, it cannot even be easily traced. But as Ngai argues in relation to tone, even though it may be a holistic phenomenon, that does not mean that its constituent parts should not be investigated, even while recognizing that the whole is not simply the sum of its parts – it is a complex, reciprocal interplay of various relations. This is a novel whose atmosphere is determined by the problems of knowledge produced by a series of crises in perspective established by the physical impairment of the narrator and, just as importantly, by the way he receives information, much of it conflicting, about his condition. The root of all these uncertainties is the sense of sight, the way that Blom's alternate conviction and uncertainty often manifests itself in the way he negotiates space – in his capacity for orientation. Thomson's writing is a particularly interesting case for such an analysis, because it simultaneously insists on and resists a holistic reading. In many ways, then, the unsettled atmosphere of *The Insult* mirrors the unsettled nature of Thomson's oeuvre as a whole.

Note

1 In the context of my present argument, these stable subject positions refer to the diegetic level of the text with only passing reference to the reader, as a full discussion would require a theorization of the reader.

Works Cited

Ahmed, Sara (2004) 'Affective Economies', *Social Text* 22(2): 117–39.

Arburg, Hans-Georg and Sergej Rickenbacher (eds) (2012) *Concordia Discors: Ästhetiken der Stimmung zwischen Literaturen, Künsten und Wissenschaften*. Würzburg: Königshausen und Neumann.

Campbell-Johnston, Rachel (1998) 'End Games', *The Times*, 14 March, LexisLibrary (consulted August 2015).

Childs, Peter and Roger Fowler (eds) (2006) *The Routledge Dictionary of Literary Terms*. Abingdon: Routledge.

Clark, Alex (2007) 'Me and a Moors Murder', *Observer*, 25 March, URL (consulted August 2015): http://www.theguardian.com/books/2007/mar/25/fiction.crimebooks

Crampton, Richard (2000) 'The Escape Artist', *The Times*, 24 June , LexisLibrary (accessed August 2015).

Davenport-Hines, Richard (1996) 'Fantasies of Seeing', *TLS*, 8 March, p. 24.

Empson, William (2004) *Seven Types of Ambiguity*. London: Pimlico.

Felski, Rita and Susan Fraiman (2012) 'Introduction', *New Literary History* 43(3): 5–12.

Gisbertz, Anna-Katharina (ed.) (2009) *Stimmung: Zur Wiederkehr einer ästhetischen Kategorie*. Munich: Fink.

Gooderham, Tim (1991) 'Devil and the deep blue sea', *TLS* (15 March): 11.

Greene, Roland et al. (eds) (2012) 'Tone', *The Princeton Encyclopedia of Poetry and Poetics*, p. 1441. Princeton, NJ: Princeton University Press.

Grossberg, Lawrence (1992) *we gotta get out of this place: popular conservatism and postmodern culture*. London: Routledge.

Gumbrecht, Hans Ulrich (2012) *Atmosphere, Mood, Stimmung: On a Hidden Potential of Literature*, trans. Erik Butler. Stanford, CA: Stanford University Press.

Highmore, Ben and Jenny Bourne Taylor (2014) 'Introducing Mood Work', *New Formations* 82: 5–12.

Koning, Christina (1999) 'The Last Word', *The Times*, 18 December, Lexis-Library (consulted August 2015).

Massumi, Brian (2002) *Parables for the Virtual: Movement, Affect, Sensation*. Durham, NC: Duke University Press.

Merritt, Stephanie (2013) '*Secrecy* by Rupert Thomson – Review', *Observer*, 23 March, URL (consulted August 2015): http://www.theguardian.com/books/2013/mar/23/secrecy-rupert-thomson-review

Myerson, Julie (2010) '*This Party's Got to Stop* – Review', *Observer*, 28 March, URL (consulted August 2015): http://www.theguardian.com/books/2010/mar/28/this-partys-got-to-stop-rupert-thomson

Neilan, Catherine (2009) 'Profiles: Rupert Thomson', *Bookseller*, 3 December, URL (consulted August 2015): http://www.thebookseller.com/profile/rupert-thomson.html

Ngai, Sianne (2005) *Ugly Feelings*. Cambridge, MA: Harvard University Press.

Rosfort, Rene and Giovanni Stanghellini (2009) 'The Person in Between Moods and Affects', *Philosophy, Psychiatry, and Psychology* 16(3): 251–66.

Thompson, Sam (2007) 'Mortuary Thoughts', *TLS* (13 April): 23.

Tilzey, Paul (1993) 'Mexican baguettes and rigid politesse: Air and fire', *Independent*, 28 May, URL (consulted August 2015): http://www.independent.co.uk/arts-entertainment/books/book-review-mexican-baguettes-and-rigid-politesse-air-and-fire-rupert-thomson-bloomsbury-pounds-1499-2316792.html

Tonkin, Boyd (2005) 'Rupert Thomson: Countries of the mind', *Independent*, 1 April, URL (consulted August 2015): http://www.independent.co.uk/arts-entertainment/books/features/rupert-thomson-countries-of-the-mind-6149237.html

Tonkin, Boyd (2010) '*This Party's Got to Stop* – Review', *Independent*, 16 April, URL (consulted August 2015): http://www.independent.co.uk/arts-entertainment/books/reviews/this-partys-got-to-stop-by-rupert-thomson-1945759.html

Wellbery, David (2000) 'Stimmung', in K. Barck et al. (eds) *Historisches Wörterbuch Ästhetischer Grundbegriffe*, pp. 703–33. Stuttgart: Metzler.

Wroe, Nicholas (2013) 'Rupert Thomson: a life in writing', *Guardian*, 8 March, URL (consulted August 2015): http://www.theguardian.com/books/2013/mar/08/robert-thomson-life-in-writing

'CANDOUR AND SECRECY'
FORMS OF FICTION IN *THIS PARTY'S GOT TO STOP* AND *SECRECY*

John McAuliffe

In his novella, 'The Figure in the Carpet' (1896), Henry James offers a brutal account of the relationship between a critic and his subject. Vereker, the novelist, condescendingly dismisses a review as 'the usual twaddle' (James, 2011: 9) without realizing that the unnamed young reviewer is within earshot. To make up for this, Vereker later accosts the reviewer and explains that he has missed entirely the 'exquisite scheme' (James, 2011: 15) as he calls it which has driven everything he has ever written. Intrigued, the reviewer devotes his time to re-reading the work, although the novelist is unforthcoming about whether he should be looking for 'an element of form or an element of feeling' (James, 2011: 17). Soon his friend Corvick and his wife-to-be are also spending far too much time on what they call '"Vereker's secret... – the general intention of his books: the string the pearls were strung on, the buried treasure, the figure in the carpet."' (James, 2011: 52):

> 'It stretches, this little trick of mine, from book to book, and everything else, comparatively, plays over the surface of it. The order, the form, the texture of my books will perhaps some day constitute for the initiated a complete representation of it. So it's naturally the thing

for the critic to look for. It strikes me,' my visitor added, smiling, 'even as the thing for the critic to find.' (James, 2011: 14)

The 'general intention' of a writer's work can now seem so suffused by the interpretation machine – the interviews and profiles and festival Q&As – that we sometimes feel as if we know a book or writer without even having to go to the trouble of reading them. My first encounter with Rupert Thomson's work was as part of that interpretation machine, soon after I arrived in Manchester, as we were beginning to put together a reading series at the university and discussing which writers we would invite to read and talk to our students. A colleague told me I should read his novels. When I suggested that we should invite him up to do a reading she baulked and then confessed that his work was so good she did not want to meet him. This might not be every novelist's idea of an ideal reader; however the split, or – better – the gap, between Thomson and his work which my colleague proposed is, it turns out, the part of his work that fascinates me and is central to the way certain images and scenes play across his novels and memoir: the originality and obliquity which characterize those repetitions draw attention to the forms of fiction he uses so carefully and originally, a sort of 'figure in the carpet' that I will, heedless of James's story, attempt to make out in the work.

Figures in the carpet

Thomson's and James's concerns with form are not of course unusual, although the emphasis on form is perhaps more often associated with poets than prose writers. Two poems with similar concerns to those in Thomson's writing, Elizabeth Bishop's 'Poem' and Thom Gunn's 'In Santa Maria del Popolo', provide productive and illuminating contexts for the effect of this formalism in Thomson's work, the latter in particular uncannily prefiguring it. First, however, I would like to set out the context for the two books of his that I will look at in this essay. Thomson's eighth book was the brilliant memoir *This Party's Got to Stop* (2010). While he is often described as a maverick or outsider by reviewers, his work, and indeed his career as a novelist, is in fact very like a slightly speeded-up version of the career of his contemporaries and peers: Hilary Mantel's memoir *Giving Up the Ghost* was her ninth book; Julian Barnes's memoir *Nothing to be Frightened of* and Jeanette Winterson's *Why Be Happy When You Could Be Normal?* each followed eight novels, while Salman Rushdie recently followed nine novels with his memoir *Joseph Anton*; Martin Amis's *Experience* also followed nine novels in 2000 with its account of his father, Kingsley, his godfather Philip Larkin, and his attempt to come to terms with their memory and the loss of his sister Sally and his cousin Lucy Partington; John McGahern's *Memoir* was his tenth book and, in a statement which relates well to this and really any discussion of the relationship between literary fiction and memoir, has been described as possibly McGahern's first truly *fictional* work.

Of these memoirs, McGahern's and Mantel's books have a similarly re-shaping imaginative propulsion towards their fictional forebears: Mantel's *Giving Up the Ghost* and McGahern's *Memoir* seem designed to make us re-read the novels which precede their memoirs in a different, challenging light. The memoirs are themselves a kind of critical foil to or even commentary on their own work, an occasionally hostile re-setting of and response to the work of their younger selves. These are perplexing and fascinating books which ask their readers to recalibrate their understanding of their authors. Mantel's family history, her illness and ghosts enter our subsequent reading (and memory) of her fiction; likewise McGahern's memoir gathers together memories of his mother who died when he was ten, and also clarifies the terrors of his childhood abuse by his father, which his readers may have anyway suspected. In both cases it is hard to avoid the feeling that they have, for better or worse, *changed* their earlier work.

There are precedents for a writer's retrospective reshaping of a corpus of work: the Victorian invention of the 'Collected Poems' has been analysed as a testamentary act by Michael Millgate (1995). These acts aimed to direct and control the readers of earlier, often less coherent work. Self-protecting and *laterself*-projecting, these collections may even seem to be written at the expense of earlier work, discarding that work, and its reception, as ingenuities and drafts of which the (older, wiser) revising authors have thought better. Does the memoir have a similarly over-riding effect on mature writers' fiction, re-casting our understanding of their fictional work with its testamentary act?

Thomson's memoir certainly does reuse material from earlier fiction. But it is not a plain restating of the factual record of events recorded differently in his fiction, as the memoir does not elide his own distinctively artful style. To frame this discussion of Thomson's memoir's relation to his fiction, it is useful to consider another writer whose work exploits the tension between life and art, a tension she had to work out in the shadow of the so-called Confessional aesthetic of her peers. Elizabeth Bishop's 'Poem', published in her final collection *Geography III* (1976), offers its own brilliant retrospect on the Nova Scotian childhood which provided material for much of her work. The poem charts Bishop's dawning recognition that she knows the place depicted in a great-uncle's 'little painting (a sketch for a larger one?)' (Bishop, 1991: 176) and has actually lived there and written about it herself, which she then proceeds to do again. 'Our visions' she writes,

> coincided – 'visions' is
> too serious a word – our looks, two looks:
> art 'copying from life' and life itself,
> life and the memory of it so compressed
> they've turned into each other. Which is which?
> Life and the memory of it cramped,
> dim, on a piece of Bristol board (Bishop, 1991: 177)

Bishop finds she can no longer tell the difference between 'life and the memory of it' in these lines, even as she adds her own reflexive, third version of the scene, 'on a piece of Bristol board'. What are we observing when 'Life and the memory of it [are] so compressed / they've turned into each other'? It's a question that challenges the reader's understanding of what is real and what is made up, or how it is we, and the writer, go about making up the real. Readers of Thomson's extraordinary memoir, which begins with a visitation ('My mother spoke to me once after she was dead' [*PGS*, 1]) and is written, mostly – and unusually for a memoir – in the present tense, may have a similar question, though at one further remove: again and again we come across scenes and images, even names, from the earlier fiction, but now as memoir. Is it possible to see them as a sort of key to the earlier work, in which the memoir acts as the key to the 'figure in the carpet' that we can then trace in the fiction?

Thomson's readers, for instance, will recognize some of the memoir's scenes from his second novel, *The Five Gates of Hell*. In that book, Thomson puts together two different narrative strands (as he did in his other early novels): one is from a hoodlum, Jed, whose point of view overlaps but does not exactly coincide with the story of Nathan, whose mother dies as the novel opens. Nathan is comforted by an aunt on his return home and his strand of the novel then tracks a fissured adolescence and a difficult if tender relationship with a sibling (a sister called George who, understandably, in light of the memoir's account of Thomson's relationship with his brothers, is reported as preferring to be his brother) and a distant and changing relationship with his father, an oddly childlike figure who subsequently marries the au pair in relation to whom the teenage Nathan negotiates troubled sexual feelings. The story will be familiar to readers of Thomson's memoir and particular scenes recur: Thomson's arrival at the family home at night and having to wake his father by throwing 'dry mud from the flower bed' at his window, so that his father descends, drowsy from his Seconal and saying 'Sorry if I look strange' (*PGS*, 12), repeats Nathan's arrival home to a locked house in the novel, waking his father with a 'handful of pebbles' so that his father emerges, 'feeling his way through some kind of thick barbiturate mist' to say 'Sorry if I look odd but I was dead out' (*FGH*, 146). Likewise, the memoir re-uses pared-back memories of massaging his father's back and the same place name 'Paradise Drive'. The novel, as will the memoir, ends with a bonfire, to which the book's evidence – videos, cheroots, stale pills and the newspaper – are consigned.

In an interview reported by Ben Saunders in 2001, Thomson spoke about the novel's experiment in autobiography:

> After his father died in February 1984, he and his two brothers (one with his wife and baby daughter) returned to the family home, where they had been born and raised, living there together for what he

called 'an extraordinary summer,' remarking, 'We had the unruliness, the untrammelled violence, of children, and yet we had no parents to control us. Everyone was dead.' [...] he originally planned on writing a novel about that summer [...] 'But within a few weeks of starting work on the book, two things happened. Firstly, I began to feel that it was too soon to be addressing such potentially explosive material. I simply did not have sufficient distance, sufficient hindsight. On a more practical level, if I had written about the experience with any degree of accuracy or truth, then it would only have served to heighten family tensions that were already running pretty high...I still have a book to write about what happened that year, but I want it to be nonfiction. It's become a secret book, one that will be written slowly and published posthumously. Three brothers return to the house where they were born following the sudden death of their father. It's material I find irresistible . . . a story that seems to have the architecture and power of a myth.' (Saunders, 2003: 267)

Ten years after the interview, however, the memoir was published. Given the intensity with which Thomson describes his troubled relationship with one of his brothers and his brother's wife, it is easy to see why he may have intended initially to publish it posthumously. Thomson is a writer who returns obsessively to similar subjects and themes (lost parents, fraternal violence and estrangement recur). In the memoir, the pattern of his narrative imagination is, perhaps, most clearly laid out. And reading it alongside *The Five Gates of Hell* generates a genuinely uncanny feeling that we have seen this before.

Of course reading through any novelist's oeuvre provides us with a constellation of repetitions and rearrangements. The bonfire is a happy ending in many of Thomson's works; the unhealthy father also recurs; newspapers are prominently binned; characters hear the voices of the dead address them; and – more centrally – the novels use the idea that the past is waiting behind us to swallow us up. This is a past which acts as a temptation Thomson's characters variously resist and give in to, trying to work out the meanings of their traumatic and often shameful experiences by attempting – and usually failing – to retell them. However, to come across his memoir and to find in it an account of material already addressed in his earlier work could seem like a coming clean rather than a variation on a theme, an explanation more than a newly imagined world. Part of the attraction of his work has been its resistance to such simplistic and reductively biographical logic, the way in which it seemed to probe the meaning of different narrative modes, offering up brilliantly imagined worlds but always naggingly reminding his readers to consider the complicated relationship between the teller and the tale as he did so.

Point of view

Recurring images can hardly be said to define Thomson's work, however. More interesting and compelling is his consistently ingenious and thoughtful manipulation of point of view. The dual narratives of his early work give way to the limited first-person narrations of *The Insult* and *The Book of Revelation* and *Death of a Murderer*: each of these books troubles the idea of reliable narration in intriguing ways. Thomson seems fascinated by the paradox that selecting a point of view will provide the motor for a story as well as its absolute limit. The blind narrator of *The Insult* may in fact be able to see everything and the book features an astonishing embedded narrative, 'Carving Babies', in which a hitherto minor character becomes central to our understanding of the present moment. As in a detective fiction, almost all of the action in the novel has already happened, and the plot is built around the slow disclosure of the past. *The Book of Revelation*, as its title suggests, also deals in revelation, and the narrator, again blinded or unable at any point to see the faces of his tormentors, searches in vain for their identity as a way to understand what they have done to him. *Death of a Murderer*, even more pertinently in this context, presents a limited first-person narrator who tells his story at an angle to a recognizable public narrative: the novel's length – a single policeman's shift – again allows for revelations and understanding of his past. Thomson's controlled, sophisticated interweaving of different parent–child or adult–child relations is a haunting achievement. Again, the novel proceeds as a detective fiction whose truth-seeking is turned away from the 'case' towards a more internal inquiry, as it slowly discovers aspects of its narrator's life, and his changing understanding of it. The narrator's febrile and occasionally hallucinatory memories are in part prompted by an apparition of Myra Hindley that appears to him, another instance of the way in which the appearance of an imagined past has real consequences for Thomson's narrators.

This Party's Got to Stop begins, as we have seen, with another apparition – literally on the same road his readers have already visited in *Five Gates of Hell*, although the memoir informs us that the road *is* actually called Paradise Drive. In the novel, the name Paradise Drive seemed as unlikely as the town's fantastical name of Moon Beach, but it does in fact exist in Eastbourne and was Thomson's childhood address. In the memoir, it is the narrator's mother who addresses him, calling out his name, from, of all things, that most funerary of trees, a yew. Her momentary presence, a year after her death, haunts and tantalizes Thomson – it is a bare reminder of what he has both lost and forgotten. The opening pages track how his bereavement leads him to the conclusion that bad things happen when his mother is not there, a thought which leads him almost unconsciously to suicidal ideation. Here, Thomson's concern with the limits of any given point of view, evident in all of his novels, is given a different force as his memoir copes with his inability to know about what has happened in his absence. The force of those absences, which so clearly influenced the development and shape of his fictions' characters, is perhaps more clearly felt in the memoir. If memoir is usually an act of witness, a first-person account of what the writer has seen, Thomson's memoir is gappy and, for the most part, uninformative. He is cautious about memory, even or especially in relation to the trauma of his mother's death: 'The darkness suddenly, and silence. I seem to remember shadowy figures at the edge of the room. I don't remember what was said' (*PGS*, 2). When he sets out to interview his extended family to uncover information about his mother and father and their life together, it is clear that he is interested in showing us how little he knew and understood, about those to whom he should have been closest, his mother and father, their extended family, the brothers with whom he grew up, and with whom he shared a house again in the wake of his father's death.

Thomson finds many brilliant images for the paralysing effect of the loss of his mother. The reader finds him visiting the tennis court where his mother died, hooking his fingers through the 'wire mesh. Grey asphalt, neat white lines'(*PGS*, 151). Later, nearby, he 'sits on a swing, pretending not to have noticed the sign that says CHILDREN UNDER 14 ONLY ... You try your utmost to get back, you can do all the imagining you want, but you can't change the fact that you weren't there' (*PGS*, 152). However, he discovers later that it was a different court on which she lay, one to which one of his mother's friends takes him. It's now a carpark. There he takes direction from his mother's tennis partner as to the exact spot on which his mother lay and ends up photographing a puddled space between a Renault and an Iveco van, noting that it looked 'empty, without a focal point ... tampered with' (*PGS*, 160). The limits of his point of view could not be clearer in these scenes, where he is physically present in significant places although his timing means he has missed the action which occurred there. Despite this, Thomson persists in his attempt to recapture if not reconstruct these formative years.

Over the course of the book Thomson interviews a number of people who knew his mother, eking out images of her which do in fact to an extent answer some of his questions. The process of uncovering that material, however, is balanced against the memoir's second major narrative, which recalls the summer he spent, twenty years later, with his brothers and sister-in-law after the death of his father. Their crazed summer has led to a continuing rift between Thomson and his youngest brother Ralph. While attempting to find out more about his mother, Thomson's research into his family tree uncovers not only a pattern of early bereavements which reflects his own situation, but also a series of fraternal rifts.

His maternal Uncle Joe, as filtered through other people's anecdotes, 'disappears behind facts, as one might disappear behind a wig and false nose' (*PGS*, 43). Uncle Joe, born Cedric, was nicknamed Joe before adopting the name Abdul Rauf, and is a good example of the way that Thomson worries away at stories until he finds a way of interpreting them and seeing their true subject. Joe's spiral from affluence via a Colombian bank, a stint in the army in Korea, a conversion to

Islam, life in a dosshouse and burial in a coffin made of fruit crates is vividly recreated (at one point Thomson does say that he had planned to make him the subject of a novel [*PGS*, 177]). Thomson's other uncle, Frank, though, cannot even remember where his brother is buried when Thomson enquires. That story, of a brother's disappearance, acts as a prompt in the memoir for Thomson's re-engagement with his estranged youngest brother Ralph.

The sense of limit, of partial perspective, is bound up with the desire to engage with other perspectives. Thomson is interested in how other people tell stories, always looking to interpret why they might tell a story or look in such a way. Frank's carelessness about his brother is presented as a culpable example of incurious narrative. If Frank is an example of a man uninterested in the past, then other characters are completely confined by it, such as his Aunt Beth who can barely move through the stockpiled newspapers, food and general junk with which she has stuffed her house and garden. Thomson offers a judicious middle way between Frank and Beth: the book acts as a kind of defence of a more curious kind of storytelling, of his own kind of enquiring, intricate and many-faceted approach to narration.

He and his youngest brother's December 2007 reunion is the climax of the book: Thomson asks Ralph about their mother and father and while this Q&A goes on, his brother guides him around shady and dilapidated areas of the city until they start doing things together, *like brothers*. The reconciliation in the present moment also seems to open up more areas of the past for Thomson, and the book ends with a brilliant closing image of him and his brother playing football on Christmas Eve, back in the same place at which the book began, though now it is not the yew tree which dominates the scene but their game which ends with the ball rolling down the road away from the house where they lived: 'The ball flies past my outstretched hand, over the gate. Luckily, no cars are going by. Standing quite still, we listen as the ball bounces off down the road. Then our eyes meet, and we laugh' (*PGS*, 263). The light, quick image of the ball rolling away seems to catch the kind of freedom for which Thomson has searched. The memoir is very aware of the different routes his life might have taken and the presence of alternative futures hangs around the margins of his book. He remembers, while stoned with his brother Robin, thinking of his father: 'Maybe we should do away with him' (*PGS*, 32). Later, their youngest brother Ralph admits that he and his wife Vivian did consider murdering *them*, by doctoring the brakes on the older brother's car. The memoir conjures these alternative lives (and deaths) without needing to pursue any one of them exclusively, and the meditative shape of the book recalibrates the scenes it reclaims from *The Five Gates of Hell*. That novel's gloved killer is now more mundanely echoed in the figure of the hearse driver (although the disastrous consummation of the relationship between the stepmother and stepson is entirely sidestepped). The earlier narrative's excesses are reined in, retooled for the memoir whose emphasis shifts from dramatic or sensational resolution to a calmer treatment of the lives it describes together.

Thomson's memoir is shaped more by pattern and image than by conventional or genre-based plot. For instance, Thomson recurrently refers to cars, which act as a sort of shorthand for characters. His Uncle Frank's self-obsession, for instance, is evident in the way he drives, 'switch[ing] lanes without signalling' and receiving 'a loud blast on the horn./"*Now* what?" Frank said' (*PGS*: 51). The car also provides Thomson with a kind of imagistic, metafictional strand of commentary on his progress, labouring in second gear along potholed Italian roads with his soon to be ex-girlfriend; forced away from any kind of vigil at his father's deathbed by the need to drive his brothers home; watching footage of motorway pile-ups with Ralph in a Shanghai massage parlour (this happens a couple of pages after he visits J. G. Ballard's Shanghai house [*PGS*, 241] which makes the allusion to *Crash* explicit); or a programme about fast cars as he lies with his brother Robin on their father's bed taking his out-of-date pills. As the three brothers finally empty their father's house, working themselves into a fine frenzy and eventually destroying furniture as they do so, it is to the soundtrack of recorded commentary of the '1958 Belgian Grand Prix' in Spa (*PGS*, 213). The other image which resonates is of his brother Robin buying two Rover 600s, one to drive and one for spare parts. And, as they drive one of the Rovers home, the gearstick comes off, which seems about right for the summer's going out of control. However it is the image of buying a second car which can be cannibalized for spare parts that acts as a metaphor for the writer's sense of the relationship between the lived and the imagined life, an image which defines this writerly memoir's rummaging through Thomson's fiction *and* memories to piece together a book about families. The memoir, which repurposes ghostly echoes of earlier fiction, interviews with witnesses, bits of travel writing, letters, recordings and, no doubt, journals of various visits, is itself a vehicle in which Thomson sets all that material on its way again, retuned and road-ready. In that closing scene, with the football rolling down the hill, Thomson notes that there were no cars coming, that the way was safe.

In the memoir's attempts to discover origins, or if not origins then patterns in his family history, it re-arranges existing fragments of Thomson's own writerly past. But the book is itself composed of fragments, and this reconstructed past, in an unusually optimistic narrative move for Thomson, changes the future of the characters for the better. His 'second look', to borrow Bishop's phrase, does not really coincide with his second novel's approach to the same familial subjects, and would, surely, have a curiously unsettling effect on readers who will find their way to *The Five Gates of Hell* via his memoir. Reading the memoir after the novel intensifies its effects, almost superseding the novel, which has a strangely confirming and enriching effect.

Fiction, after memoir

The memoir's cannibalization of his fiction raised a question about how Thomson would write his next novel. How have other writers managed? Perhaps the most pertinent example is Hilary Mantel who followed *Giving Up the Ghost* first with a book about a psychic who attempts, among other things, to reconstruct a traumatic childhood. Told through the points of view of the psychic and her business partner Colette, this is a sort of 'family' novel which was followed, of course, by two historical novels about the birth of a nation (and a royal family). These novels aim to reconstruct traumatic origins and they are characterized by their unusual point of view, that of the almost omniscient spymaster Thomas Cromwell. For Mantel, the memoir and its successor, *Beyond Black*, generate a mode of narrative which is confident and driven in the way it represents the past as a necessary way of imagining the future. Like *Wolf Hall*, Thomson's *Secrecy* is a historical novel published directly after the memoir, and like *Wolf Hall*, *Secrecy* tracks an outsider's path through court intrigues and violent religious controversy, although Thomson's narrator is closer to the frustrated seer Alison in *Beyond Black* than the spymaster through whose eyes we see events unfold in *Wolf Hall*. Thomson's novel is also a romance and a meditation on art; its strong narrative plot is offset by a kind of ekphrastic consideration of what it is we do when we frame and re-present a subject. The memoir's resolutions and revelations do not exactly repudiate the mysteries and blank spaces of which fictions make us aware. In fact, *Secrecy* returns us directly to such mysteries: the backstory of warring brothers in his memoir feels charged by Thomson's return to it as a cause for the creativity of *Secrecy's* protagonist Zummo. More generally, readers of his memoir will be familiar with his emphasis on the limits of point of view. The novel's questions about authority and the power of story-telling restate Thomson's relativist emphasis on the importance of form and narrative shape in how any representation will be understood.

The main narrative in *Secrecy* concerns the artist/anatomist Zummo whose wax models of decaying bodies attract the patronage of a Florentine duke. This historical novel may well resemble Florence c. 1701 but it is also familiar terrain to Thomson's readers. Zummo, like many Thomson characters, is constantly looking over his shoulder, and rumours of his origins and past – which includes a difficult relationship with his brother – give ammunition to his enemies and propel their plots against him. Florence is imagined as a sort of police state, not very dissimilar to the worlds imagined in *Divided Kingdom* and *The Insult*. He befriends a circus performer (as does the central character of *The Insult*, another man with whom the past catches up). However, there are other elements of the novel which signal Thomson's presence. For no particular reason, he renames the artist

Zumbo as Zummo (an odd dropped consonant which must chime with the dropped 'p' with which Thomson changed his name from Thompson), and the artist's age – he is 55 at the time he begins to tell his story, which is also Thomson's age at the time of writing the novel. A reader's interest in the novel's naming of its protagonists is prompted by the book's villain, a monk named Stufa, an anagram of Faust, while Zummo's lover is named Faustina. Zummo's career as a maker of wax grotesques may be a closer match to Thomson's YBA (Young British Artists) contemporaries, but the length of Zummo's career and its peripatetic nature also bear some resemblance to Thomson's. His emphasis on Zummo's art and his commission to create a wax figure, a beautiful woman with a secret – a foetus which Zummo hides in her body – resembles Thomson's own narrative interest in telling a story which is different to its ostensible subject, and whose point is revealed more by the way in which it is narrated than by what is actually told to us. Thomson is emphatic too about Zummo's commitment to verisimilitude and the lengths to which he must go to find fresh corpses on which his work will be modelled.

The novel's frame narrative is a brief encounter in 1701 between Zummo and Marguerite-Louise, estranged wife of the Grand Duke, now resident in a convent. Her point of view is where we begin and at first as she looks at the arriving carriage, she can see very little: 'The door opened a few inches. Closed again. Then opened wide.' (*Se*, 3) She comments on the appearance of Zummo – sick (she can 'sense the bones beneath the skin' [*Se*, 7]), in worn clothes – and on his writing style ('using more words than were strictly necessary'), before his revelation, about her secret daughter, makes her 'feel as if I was whirling backward. The walls of the present gave, and the past flowed in – turbulent, irrepressible, choked with debris' (*Se*, 7). The characteristic image Thomson then reaches for typically mixes together a particular moment and the consciousness through which we see it: 'Outside the rain was slanting down like vicious pencil strokes, as if the bleak landscape east of Paris was a mistake that somebody was crossing out' (*Se*, 7). It is a classic Thomson opening scene, and it is the scene, after almost 300 pages of the main retrospective Zummo narrative, to which the reader must return. The shape of the novel, then, is quite unusual, but it also cleverly mimics the wax figure Zummo makes for the Duke: the hidden child becomes one of the book's central characters. In a way that is different to the memoir, where we learn about events at the same pace as the narrator, in Thomson's fictions central characters are separated from the 'sighted' perspective of his readers, who realize, by way of Thomson's use of dramatic irony, that the characters cannot know the truth that their stories embody.

Thomson's themes and even his setting bear an uncanny resemblance to a poem by his part-namesake Thom Gunn. Gunn's ekphrastic poem 'In Santa Maria del Popolo' is just as concerned as Thomson is with the ways in which masks offer ways into treating difficult autobiographical material. Gunn too is a self-reflexive and self-conscious stylist who is just as interested in foregrounding the ways in which masks generate a way of reflecting on the forms of representation, the ways in which a story is told. The poem imagines a life in the shadows, a response to Caravaggio's painting of Saul being blinded, in that short period before he becomes Paul, having been healed by Ananias. The image is housed in the church of the poem's title where 'shadow in the painting brims / With a real shadow, drowning all shapes out' (Gunn, 1993: 93). Addressing Caravaggio, Gunn writes:

> O wily painter, limiting the scene
> From a cacophony of dusty forms
> To the one convulsion, what is it you mean
> In that wide gesture of the lifting arms? (Gunn, 1993: 93)

Gunn then credits the image as an example of something else, a covert image, not of Saul, or Paul, but an image of the life Caravaggio knew, his models drawn from the 'whores' and 'cheats' he 'picked off the streets':

> The painter saw what was, an alternate
> Candour and secrecy inside the skin. (Gunn, 1993: 93)

The poem then shifts its attention away from the painting to its setting, the church whose congregation prays, 'each head closeted in tiny fists' (Gunn, 1993: 94). Reading *Secrecy*, Gunn's poem can seem to prefigure the novel's concerns with form, as well as its actual plot: its juxtaposition of 'candour and secrecy inside the skin' describes Thomson's concerns very well, with its puzzled apprehension of the mysterious facts of the world and the sense that this is more than enough subject matter without needing to draw upon a religious myth by which it could alternatively be read and comprehended.

In the same way that Thomson returned to early fiction in later autobiographical writing, Gunn writes very differently at the beginning and ending of his life about the death of his mother (who died, by suicide, soon after her divorce from Gunn's father). It is only, in fact, in the final collection *Boss Cupid* that Gunn discloses his mother's suicide in a poem called 'The Gas Poker', a poem whose images suddenly alter our understanding of earlier poems which now come into focus as responses to her death. Another of Gunn's responses to this terrible trauma was to reject his given name, which was William, and take instead his mother's maiden name – Thomson, by uncanny coincidence – as his name instead, a choice of an identity and an insistence on agency which is predicated on the loss of identity and of agency.

Gunn is, it seems to me, very interested in the way that *wily* Caravaggio can 'cover' well-known material on his own terms, yoking the conversion of Saul – as painted by Raphael, Michelangelo, Cranach and many others, including on at least one other occasion himself – into a different context, using shadow and light to show us the blind soldier flat on his back, the horse's hoof poised nearby and the man himself 'embracing' – 'embracing what?' Gunn asks, before he himself turns this material to his own ends, swinging the painting into his own re-imagination of identity, desire and sexuality. In the last stanza, he plays off an ironic reference to enlightenment and also, as he imagines those who pray in the church where the painting is housed with each head 'closeted / in tiny fists holds comfort as it can', describing the scene at the same time as he asks readers to dwell more broadly on what he might mean by 'closeted'.

Gunn's ekphrastic poem challenges the static image of the painting and, even as it assumes its own formal shape, insists instead on the temporizing narrative possibilities of writing, classically dividing painting and writing, seeing them as rival rather than sister arts. Gunn, though, respects the imminence of painting, what he calls the 'candour and secrecy inside the skin' of Caravaggio's image, an image which has the capacity to prompt and regenerate new thoughts and feelings in its viewer. Gunn's poem is suggestive rather than exhaustive in its treatment of the image. Likewise, Thomson's ekphrastic response to Zummo's wax bodies, even as it retains the same 'figure in the carpet' as his earlier novels and memoir, expands his interest in the limitations of narrative. Thomson shares Gunn's fascination with the ways in which art affects or contrives its point of view, its place of narration, and how this itself has an effect on readers or viewers. These are the works of writers who have accrued authority by publication, but whose later work begins to rethink and re-use, sometimes critically, the gambits and forms of their original authority. How, then, do we read Thomson's 2015 novel, *Katherine Carlyle*? Its protagonist is a motherless child, who sets off, abandoning her remaining family, through continental Europe. Thomson's readers will read on, already having a sense of what is at stake in such separations, and wondering how exactly he will tease out new meanings and outcomes from this familiar journey.

Works Cited

Amis, Martin (2000) *Experience*. London: Cape.
Barnes, Julian (2008) *Nothing to Be Frightened Of*. London: Vintage.
Bishop, Elizabeth (1991) *Complete Poems*. London: Chatto.
Gunn, Thom (1993) *Collected Poems*. London: Faber.
James, Henry (2011) *The Figure in the Carpet*. Auckland: Floating Press.
McGahern, John (2005) *Memoir*. London: Faber.
Mantel, Hilary (2003) *Giving up the Ghost*. London: Fourth Estate.
Mantel, Hilary (2005) *Beyond Black*. London: Fourth Estate.
Mantel, Hilary (2009) *Wolf Hall*. London: Fourth Estate.
Millgate, Michael (1995) *Testamentary Acts: Browning, Tennyson, James, Hardy*. Oxford: Oxford University Press.
Rushdie, Salman (2012) *Joseph Anton: A Memoir*. London: Jonathan Cape.
Saunders, Ben (2003) 'Rupert Thomson', in Michael R. Molino (ed.) *Dictionary of Literary Biography: Twenty-first-Century British and Irish Novelists*, Vol. 267, pp. 322–9. Detroit, MI: Gale.
Winterson, Jeanette (2011) *Why Be Happy When You Could Be Normal?* London: Vintage.

NOTES ON CONTRIBUTORS

Robert Duggan is Senior Lecturer in English Literature at the University of Central Lancashire. He is the author of *The Grotesque in Contemporary British Fiction* (MUP, 2013). He has published widely on modern British literature and his research explores experiments in literary form and genre in the work of writers including Martin Amis, Ian McEwan, Angela Carter, Will Self, Iain Banks, Toby Litt and China Miéville.

Rhona Gordon completed her PhD at the University of Glasgow with her thesis entitled 'Housing Matters in the Texts of Gordon Burn, Andrew O'Hagan and David Peace.' She has published on Burn, Peace and O'Hagan and is currently turning her thesis into a monograph. Her research interests include working-class British fiction, representations of late twentieth century housing and twenty/twenty-first century celebrity.

John McAuliffe is Reader in Modern Literature and Creative Writing at the University of Manchester. He has published four poetry collections, his book *Of All Places* was a Poetry Book Society Recommendation for autumn 2011. John's poems have appeared in *The Guardian*, *Irish Times* and many literary journals. He co-founded Manchester's Centre for New Writing, and writes a monthly poetry column for *The Irish Times*. His most recent collection, *The Way In*, was published in 2015.

Kaye Mitchell is Senior Lecturer in Contemporary Literature at the University of Manchester. She is the author of *A.L. Kennedy* (Palgrave,

2007) and *Intention and Text* (Continuum, 2008), and edited *Sarah Waters* (Bloomsbury, 2013) and a special issue of *Contemporary Women's Writing* on experimental writing (2015). Her work in progress includes a monograph on the politics and poetics of shame in contemporary literature (for which she received a Humboldt Experienced Researcher Fellowship) and a co-edited collection on British avant-garde writing of the 1960s.

Rebecca Pohl is Honorary Research Fellow at the University of Manchester where she works on a Leverhulme project on aesthetics. Rebecca's research is situated at the intersection of contemporary literature and women's writing, with a particular focus on literary institutions and discourses of literary value. Her current project looks at experimental women's writing, especially the relationship between pleasure, accessibility and difficulty. Rebecca has published on Sarah Waters and Victorian visual culture. She translates theory and poetry.

Iain Robinson is Tutor at the University of East Anglia. He holds a PhD in Creative and Critical Writing from the University of East Anglia. His book chapter on Sarah Hall's *The Carhullan Army* appeared in *What Happens Now* (Palgrave, 2013) and his article on Will Self's *The Book of Dave* is published in the journal *C21 Literature* (Gylphi, 2013). His short fiction has appeared in *Litro Magazine, The Missing Slate, The Lonely Crowd*, and the short story anthologies *Hearing Voices* (Litro, 2015) and *Being Dad* (Tangent, 2016). He is on the editorial team of *Lighthouse Journal*.

Christopher Vardy is completing a PhD exploring figurations of Thatcherism and the End of History in twenty-first-century British fiction. He has previously published journal articles on contemporary American fiction and dystopian/abusive narratives about the recent past, as well as book chapters on the politics of nostalgia and childhood.

INDEX